Effective College and University Teaching

A Practical Guide

Eleanor Boyle
Harley Rothstein

Library and Archives Canada Cataloguing in Publication

Boyle, Eleanor A., 1953-
Essentials of college and university teaching : a practical guide / Eleanor Boyle and Harley Rothstein.—2nd rev. ed.

Includes bibliographical references and index.
ISBN 1-894694-42-2

1. College teaching. 2. Effective teaching.
I. Rothstein, Harley, 1946- II. Title.

LB2331.B69 2006   378.1'25   C2005-906818-3

Book designer: Suzi Shack
Cover design: Shelley Wales
Proofreader: Neall Calvert

Second revised edition 2006
Printed in Canada

⊓

Granville Island
P u b l i s h i n g
212–1656 Duranleau
Vancouver, BC, Canada V6H 3S4
Tel: (604) 688-0320 Toll free: 1-877-688-0320
www.GranvilleIslandPublishing.com

Contents

Class Planning: Being Thoroughly Organized for Each Session

Communication: Striving for Clarity

Management: Developing Techniques for Smoothly Functioning Classes

Evaluation: Assessing Student Work Fairly

Conclusion: Reflecting On Our Teaching

Acknowledgments

Our heartfelt thanks to the many people who contributed to the making of this book, including our mentors and colleagues who were so generous with their time and ideas. We apologize to them for whatever weaknesses the book may have, whether omissions or errors of judgment or fact.

First, our own mentors who inspired us by their commitment to excellence in teaching. They include Jim Winter, William Bruneau, J. Donald Wilson, Jean Barman, Neil Sutherland, Ed Hundert, Sandra Davies, Cecily Overall, Dave Wirtshafter, Campbell Clark, Pat McGeer, and the late John Stark.

Our deep thanks to colleagues who read all or parts of the manuscript and who contributed detailed comments and valuable ideas: Leonard Angel, Robert Campbell, Gary Poole, Alan Morris, Chris Gratham, Peter Seixas, Sandra Bruneau, and Selma Wassermann. Thank you also to Paul Avery, Cara Zaskow, Michael MacNeill, Janet Waters, Sandra Moe, Rosalie Hawrylko, Karen Ewing, and Gary Mangel, who contributed beneficial suggestions.

Thank you to other colleagues and teachers from whom we have received encouragement and learned a great deal: Alan Clingman, Ron MacGregor, Bill Kirkman, Joanne Weinberg, Jim Ogloff, Jay McGilvery, Claudia Beaven, Marlene LeGates, Towser Jones, Bob Muckle, Melanie Fahlman-Reid, Bill Willmott,

Maurice Gibbons, John Ellis, Jim McPherson, Jack Gammer, Andy Burt, Peter Welton, Will Foster, Matthew Oram, Gary Armour, and Peter McLean.

We also want to thank Wilbert J. McKeachie, whose book *McKeachie's Teaching Tips* was so useful for us when we first taught university.

Thank you to our publisher, Jo Blackmore, for her enthusiasm about this project, her attention to detail, her good taste, and her accommodation of our many preferences. We thank Suzi Shack, Neall Calvert, Heather Young, and Fernanda Viveiros for their skilful and good-natured approach to text design, proofreading, and production. We extend appreciation to our expert graphic artist, Shelley Wales, for her work on the cover. Thank you to Al Karim and his staff for technical assistance.

For production assistance on an earlier edition of this book we thank Mary Schendlinger, Linda Field, and Carol Hamshaw. Thank you to Stan and Miriam Fisher for other suggestions and encouragement.

Our deepest thanks and appreciation to friends and family for their support, love, and teaching by example over the years, particularly Annette Rothstein, the late Norman Rothstein, Marjorie and Tom Boyle, Kris Rothstein, Sam Macklin, John Munro, Debbie Weinstein, Linda Nading, and Daniel and Hanna Siegel.

We also thank our thousands of students over the years for their enthusiasm and commitment to learning. They are the ultimate reason for our writing this book.

Foreword

Becoming an outstanding instructor at the college or university level requires a great deal of hard work and dedication. In return, teaching offers many rewards, including that there is no better way to learn a subject than to teach it to others. A thorough knowledge of the relevant material, however, is not the only requirement for being an effective instructor. Teaching itself is a skill that has to be learned.

Observing other instructors, and learning from personal experience, play essential roles in the development of professorial skills. Nevertheless, professors can also learn a great deal from direct instruction. The same sorts of organizational and pedagogical issues come up again and again in different courses, and learning how others have dealt with them can be of immeasurable assistance. Well-chosen guidance from experienced individuals can help point teachers in the right direction, help them avoid potential problems before they develop, and assist them in maximizing their instructional efficiency.

Boyle and Rothstein's book *Effective College and University Teaching* aims to provide such guidance. I think that it succeeds admirably. The authors clearly love to teach and they tackle the difficult topic of "teaching teaching" with infectious energy and great effectiveness. This book would be a wonderful guide for the beginning instructor, or for the advanced graduate student who is about to embark on a teaching career. It makes for very informative reading in its own right, but it would also serve quite well as a text or supplement in a course on teaching techniques, which are becoming quite common in many graduate programs.

As a glance at the table of contents will prove, the book addresses a tremendous variety of topics, ranging from structural issues, such as the construction of exams and the writing of syllabi, to more "stylistic" topics, offering advice on such things as the best way to prepare and deliver lectures and the most effective techniques for providing students with feedback.

Picasso said that good artists borrow, but great artists steal. The same may well hold true for teachers! This book is packed with good ideas and tips that are worth stealing. I wish it had been available when I started out—it would have made things much easier for me, and I'm sure, would have enhanced the educational experience of many of my students. I have been teaching at the University of Illinois at Chicago for more than 25 years now, and have won a number of teaching awards, but I felt that I learned a great deal from reading this book. I am sure that my experience in this regard will not be unique.

David R. Wirtshafter, PhD,
Professor of Behavioral Neuroscience,
University of Illinois at Chicago
Excellence in Teaching Award recipient,
University of Illinois, 2002

Introduction:

Teaching Stretches the Mind, the Heart, and the Soul

Chapter 1

All Instructors Can Learn to Teach Effectively

When I taught my first college class, I was thrilled at the opportunity, but very nervous. After all, as a graduate student in a Ph.D. program, I had received no training in how to be an effective instructor. I wanted to be a good teacher, but wasn't certain I'd be competent to lead, inform, and inspire, not to mention judge students' efforts with a letter-grade that might affect their lives. – EB

Good teachers are not just born; for the most part they are made. While a few exceptional individuals may be naturals in the classroom, most high-quality instruction doesn't happen by magic. The school system understands this and requires that those who want to teach 7-year-olds or 17-year-olds complete demanding teacher-training programs. But it has been different in the post-secondary system, where individuals who aspire to teach 18-year-olds or 28-year-olds have been required to learn little of the art and science of transmitting knowledge effectively. To obtain a faculty position at most colleges and universities we must have earned advanced degrees in specific subject areas. But in many cases we need not have completed even a weekend seminar in teaching methods and techniques. While many post-secondary faculty are excellent instructors, most have had to teach themselves how to teach. The situation is improving as universities set up instructional-development offices and begin to ask for teaching credentials and experience as part of job applicants' files. But to a large degree the assumption remains that people who are experts in their disciplines will automatically teach those disciplines well. We disagree.

We also question the idea that, because adult students are mature and motivated, teaching well is unnecessary. On the contrary, we believe that no matter how intelligent and keen our students, they hunger for us to teach as well as we can. They want and need us to plan our courses thoroughly, present the material in an organized and comprehensible fashion, help motivate them to be excited about the material, and evaluate them fairly.

Good teaching requires that an individual cultivate certain underlying qualities. These include knowledge of the academic material, positive attitudes toward students, and an enthusiasm for the learning enterprise. But even these prerequisites are no guarantee. Excellent instruction requires the development of specific teaching skills and methods that are finite, identifiable, and acquirable. They involve strategies for planning and organization, communication, classroom management, motivation, and student evaluation. These are the essentials of teaching, and they are applicable at any level from elementary to graduate school. These instructional fundamentals also apply to non-academic settings, whether for teaching time-management to executives or yoga to senior citizens. The skills are similar whether you are making a one-time presentation or teaching a year-long course.

Teaching is therefore an activity that stretches the mind, not just to understand the academic material but to develop instructional approaches and strategies. That is not to say that teaching is a mechanical activity or even an entirely intellectual one. As will be discussed in the next chapter, excellent instruction requires the heart as well as the head. But good teaching is based on a foundation of principles that can be learned.

Many college and university instructors successfully promote productive learning environments and kindle student interest in the life of the mind. But anyone who has attended university knows that some instructors do not teach well, that a few are uninteresting, disorganized, or unclear. Students are in no position to demand excellent teaching since they are evaluated by the very providers of that education. When students feel unhappy, they are usually reluctant to complain. Often constrained by geography or funding, they do not have endless choices of institutions to attend. Higher education is not an ideal free market for students as consumers.

Neither does the system operate in the best interests of instructors, all of whom would like to teach well. As most people in the academic world (but too few outside that world) realize, universities generally reward faculty for high-quality academic research, not for high-quality teaching. As a result, university faculty are pressured to spend most of their time on research and only marginal hours on teaching.[1] A few years ago an influential university department head made a memorable remark to one of us regarding hiring criteria. "We hire faculty based on research brilliance," he said, "and teaching adequacy."

Post-secondary instructors who are determined to teach well persevere and train themselves on the job. They use a variety of tactics. They recall what excited them as students, and think about what constitutes good teaching. They observe others whose teaching they admire. They take risks in the classroom with new techniques, ideas, and exercises. They observe what works and what doesn't, and make adjustments next time around.

Many instructors also find time to attend teaching seminars, of which increasing numbers are available at colleges and universities. We are optimistic about the movement in higher education today to offer workshops, mentoring programs to faculty, training to teaching assistants, and other teaching-support services. One active faculty development group calls itself POD—the Professional and Organizational Development Network in Higher Education. Based in the United States, POD supports professors and instructors in their teaching, and advocates for greater emphasis on quality instruction in post-secondary institutions. In Canada, the Society for Teaching and Learning in Higher Education (STLHE) sponsors initiatives including an annual conference, prestigious instructional awards, and other programs to enhance the value placed on teaching and learning at universities.[2] Increasingly, faculty members are participating in what has come to be called the scholarship of teaching, in which systematic research is conducted on how professors can teach, and students can learn, most effectively.

Meanwhile, we believe that many more resources are needed to assist both beginning and experienced instructors. One reason we have written this book is that we could have used it ourselves, and could still use it today. Such a handbook would have been valuable for advice on how to solve a teaching problem, or for a novel idea when we had temporarily lost our inspiration.

In these pages we present a body of teaching principles, applicable at numerous levels and in numerous teaching situations. We believe that the book will be useful for a wide range of readers. It's for the first-year instructor who feels excited but unprepared to teach university classes. It's for the professor who has been teaching for five years and realizes s/he has never systematically learned instructional techniques. It's for the instructor who has been teaching for 10 to 15 years but is feeling stale and needs some new ideas. It's also for the veteran professor who could use a few reminders.

Though both of us have learned the majority of our teaching skills in the classroom as well as from mentors and colleagues, Harley also has had the benefit of formal teacher training. As an education instructor and supervisor, he has spent hundreds of hours at the backs of classrooms observing the teaching process, analyzing and making extensive notes on what constitutes good practice. Eleanor has led numerous instructional workshops for faculty and has discovered the extent to which our colleagues want practical ideas and strategies that they can apply in the classroom immediately. Together we have taught for more than 30 years at a variety of levels from elementary school, to college and university undergraduate, to post-graduate. We have taught in the arts, the sciences, and professional school, and believe that teaching fundamentals transcend disciplines.

While much of this book consists of what we would call teaching principles, it also contains points of view that we have developed through experience. Not everyone will agree entirely with our perspective. But we trust that the book will be useful nonetheless. Underlying our work is our philosophy of teaching, which can be summarized as follows:

- Human relations in teaching and learning should be governed by respect and compassion.
- The foundation of good teaching is thorough preparation and organization.
- Teaching is composed mainly of an identifiable set of skills and attitudes that can be learned.
- Informative and interesting lectures should be combined with frequent and meaningful opportunities for students to interact with the course material and with each other.
- Effective communication and questioning techniques are key components of good teaching.
- Evaluation of students should be governed by fairness, transparency, and rigour.
- Instructors should find ways to include all students and to treat each one as an individual.
- Students should be encouraged to critically evaluate information and to express opinions about the ideas presented in the course.
- Student suggestions about the course material and its presentation should be carefully considered, but responsibility for the success of a course rests with the instructor.
- The teacher's primary task is to transmit knowledge, skills, and attitudes. But the teacher's job is also inspirational, to convey enthusiasm for the specific material and for the learning enterprise.

We encourage you to think about and develop your own teaching philosophy even though it may differ in emphasis or even principle from those of your colleagues. Many different approaches and personal styles can result in excellent teaching.

Most teaching ideas are ultimately derivative, obtained from some source long ago. You hear a useful-sounding idea from a colleague who heard the idea from someone else, so you try it with your students, and adapt it over numerous semesters. Five years later, you cannot remember where you got the idea in the first place. This process occurs often in teaching, which is a collaborative enterprise. We too are not always certain of the origins of our methods, which rely partly on the genius and hard work of others who have taught before. We're delighted to share in this information network, of which you are also a part. If you derive useful ideas from this book, and five years from now don't remember their source, that's fine with us! In turn, if you have suggestions to share, or comments to make, we warmly welcome your e-mails or letters.

The lessons in this book are ones we have personally learned, sometimes the hard way. Some of the mistakes we discuss are ones we still occasionally make. When we do, we remind ourselves of the teaching essentials and remember our good fortune in being able to pursue this worthy work.

Chapter 2

Learning Environments are Based on Compassion and Respect

Teaching is an activity not only of the head, but of the heart. If we are to be effective facilitators of learning, our teaching must be based on attitudes of compassion and respect—toward ourselves, toward students, and toward others outside the classroom. Our teaching must be based on empathy for ourselves and for students, wanting the best for them as human beings and as learners.

First, show compassion and respect toward yourself. Identify in yourself your best personal qualities, which will then shine through in the classroom. You will want students to experience your confidence without conceit, and humility without self-deprecation. Your attitudes toward yourself and toward teaching will be evident every day. One interesting phenomenon of teaching is that your students get to know a good deal about you even if you don't say a single word about yourself, just by listening to the words you choose, watching your body language, and hearing your tone of voice. By these cues they come to know your personality, your competencies, and your attitudes, whether you are intimidating or inviting, an adversary or an advocate.

Then, be confident in your professional skills and abilities. You are capable of establishing an excellent learning environment. It is within your power to create a good class or a poor one. The quality

9

of your class is not determined primarily by the personalities of students, the scheduled time of your sessions, the room you were assigned, or other such factors. Not that these are irrelevant. But the quality of your classes is largely within your control.

Try to overcome perfectionist tendencies. Teaching is like parenting: flawlessness is impossible, mistakes inevitable. Demand high-quality work of yourself, but be forgiving. Do your best and realize that students are resilient. For example, your first attempts at participatory methods may not work as well as you would like. But there's no rule against stopping an activity halfway through with: "Students, this isn't accomplishing what I had hoped. Let's stop for now. We'll try it differently next time." And move back to lecturing. Back in your office, analyze the activity, determine how to improve it, and congratulate yourself for trying. Don't give up efforts to broaden your repertoire because a first attempt wasn't perfect.

Show respect for yourself by not allowing disruptive behaviour in class. Avoid raising your voice to speak over whisperers in the back row. We suggest that you not tolerate persistent talking and laughing among a few students. Show that you deserve respect and that you require it. Then, extend compassion and respect toward students. Remind yourself that they are intelligent and motivated. The vast majority want to be at university and want to learn. Give students the benefit of the doubt. If a few don't purchase the required textbook, do not assume they're unmotivated. Maybe they can't afford it. Education is expensive and not easily available to all students. If you ask a question in class and students don't respond, do not assume they are unintelligent or devoid of ideas. You probably asked the wrong question—one that is too big, too small, confusing, or uninteresting. The classroom is an unnaturally formal environment that encourages passivity. Have empathy for students who are put in a dull physical space and then asked to be creative. They need you to provide a learning environment that allows them to express their opinions, ideas, and abilities. Resist blaming students if your classes are not going well. That is not to say you should blame yourself, just that students are in a position of relative powerlessness, dependent on you to set the tone. However, you can remind students that they should take responsibility for their learning and for the grades they earn. Teaching at its best is a cooperative effort in which all parties have reasonable expectations of each other.

Never laugh at, or show disrespect to, individual students. Deference may not be what it once was, but do not underestimate the power of the professor to hurt or to help.

Encourage a variety of opinions in the classroom. This will enliven discussion, model tolerance and respect for diversity, and demonstrate to students the necessity for all of us to challenge ourselves. As part of this quest, we believe it is important to allow and even encourage the expression of unfashionable opinions. A few years ago in Eleanor's class, during a discussion of marriage and gender roles, one young woman voiced the opinion that a man should be the indisputable head of the household with the final say in family decisions. Other students appeared surprised; no-one knew what to say. In our opinion, most polemical statements from students demand response from the instructor. The response can acknowledge the controversial nature of the opinion but should do so respectfully. In this case we suggest something like: "Many students will disagree and say that equality of decision-making is important in a partnership. But there may be people who agree with you, unpopular as this view is today. What's important is that both partners understand and agree on the ground-rules for their relationship, and that no-one feels they are being abused or oppressed."

Is it wise to let class members know where you stand on controversial issues? We say a cautious yes. The best teachers realize they hold points of view that influence their treatment of the academic material and even affect the way they organize a course. On occasion it is reasonable to inform students of those points of view. At the same time, instructors should make it clear that students are not required to agree with them to do well in the course. It is also important that instructors acknowledge major contending theories or perspectives held by other scholars, along with supporting arguments, so learners can consider a variety of intellectual positions.

Just as you show respect for students, encourage students to show respect for each other. Avoid allowing participants to gang up on one member of the class who has made an unpopular statement. On the other hand, we believe instructors should not let offensive comments go unanswered. If one student has voiced an opinion that is racist, sexist, homophobic, or otherwise demeaning to an individual or a group, make it clear that such comments are unacceptable. We favour the direct but compassionate approach, for example: "I appreciate your being willing to express your opinion, but comments that demean any group are not acceptable in this classroom. You probably didn't intend your comment that way, but some people may interpret it as hurtful." Your institution probably has guidelines to which you can refer. You may want to set rules of conduct, especially if you frequently deal with controversial topics. A set of ground rules might include:

- I respect others' rights to hold opinions different from mine, and understand that people may have a variety of points of view that have been arrived at genuinely and thoughtfully.
- I agree to listen carefully, with an open mind, to other people's stated opinions.
- I will attempt to state my opinions in ways that will not offend others.
- If I disagree with an individual's opinion, I will express myself without criticizing the individual herself/himself.

Your compassion and respect will extend to those outside the classroom, and you will probably want students' attitudes to do the same. Demonstrate respect for your colleagues and your institution. In speaking with students, avoid criticizing your co-workers. This can be tricky when you clearly disagree with one or more of those. The issue can also arise if a student believes you have contradicted another instructor, for example: "You're telling us that pharmacological immunosuppression is necessary in these surgeries, but Professor Lee told us in our other class that it isn't always needed. Who's right?"

Such discrepancies may be mere matters of terminology, in which you the historian used a different term for a phenomenon than your colleague the sociologist did. Once again, compassion for students is in order. It is frustrating for them that instructors in different disciplines do not always speak the same language. When the discrepancy is not so easy to sort out, you can take several possible approaches.

(a) Thank students for pointing out the apparent contradiction, and say you will check with your colleague and get back to them on it. Often students have remembered incorrectly.

(b) Tell them the apparent contradiction is an example of two different approaches to an issue, either of which is valid and reasonable.

(c) Buy time to think, and come back next time with a restatement of the issue that preserves the credibility of both your colleague and yourself. Needless to say, if you're out-and-out wrong, if you made a statement that in retrospect you wish you had not, be honest and say so. Restate the issue clearly, apologize, and move on.

Showing respect for your university or college can be dodgy when you strongly disagree with institutional policies. We believe it is acceptable to voice reservations about such-and-such a divisional policy or departmental decision; in any well-meaning group of individuals not everyone is going to agree. A basic principle of feedback is relevant here: just as you would gently criticize a student's idea but not the student personally, so you can criticize the policy but not the department or institution itself.

Values

Our values are implicit in our teaching. This point is most overt in the humanities and social sciences that deal directly or indirectly with issues about which people have strong opinions, often related to their day-to-day lives. But it is also true in other disciplines, in the physical sciences that communicate strong world-views about technology and progress, and in professional schools where ethics and accepted conduct are discussed. Our beliefs and priorities emerge in the classroom in our expressed attitudes and in the way we treat students and others, whether we explicitly teach values or not.

Of course, adult students are less impressionable than children and can choose to reject our values whatever those may be. Most students realize that we hold our academic positions by virtue of our expertise in the Italian Renaissance or geological engineering, not our expertise in living well. Nevertheless, as experts and as role models we sometimes unwittingly project authority in realms other than our areas of expertise, and transmit the values that we act out.

What specific values do you want to teach? You might list those that are important to you. These may involve tolerance and equal opportunity, skepticism without cynicism, the importance of objective intellectual inquiry, and the merit of being an informed citizen.

In most organizations, attitudes start from the top. As the instructor, you will set the tone for the interactions in your classroom. That tone will be shaped by your commitment to values such as compassion and respect.

Chapter 3

To Teach Well, Remember the Essentials

In athletics, when you lose your edge partway through a competition, you can often pull out of a slump by clearing your head and reminding yourself of the essentials. In tennis, for example, when you lose your precision and start hitting balls into the net, it helps to recall what your first tennis teacher told you, which went something like: Keep your eye on the ball, get your racket back early, hit the ball out in front, be on your toes and get into position, and follow through. Teaching is similar.

In tennis . . .	In teaching . . .
Keep your eye on the ball.	Course planning: Having a strong overall vision.
Get your racket back early.	Class planning: Being thoroughly organized for each session.
Hit the ball out in front.	Communication: Striving for clarity.
Be on your toes and get into position.	Management: Developing techniques for smoothly functioning classes.
Follow through.	Evaluation: Assessing student work fairly.

The athletics analogy produces a beautiful little set of guidelines that can apply to many aspects of life, including teaching. Teaching has its own essentials that we identify as course planning, class planning, communication, management, and evaluation.

Of course there is more to any complex pursuit than a few brief maxims. But basic principles form the foundation of most important activities. We are reminded of this by the many spiritual and wisdom traditions that encourage us to see through the complexity of life to find the simplicity within.

Teaching can indeed be experienced as a spiritual activity. At its best it nourishes the soul through its purposefulness, opening minds of younger generations for creativity and continuity. Teaching also demands humility similar to how we all feel in the face of human limitation. Teaching can never be done perfectly. We instructors often make mistakes, and sometimes have a run of them. But we continue because the exercise is one worthy of our effort and our time.

Teaching also requires calm and concentration on the here-and-now. If we race from the parking lot into the office at 8:25 a.m., then to an 8:30 class, it is difficult to feel ready to teach because the other concerns of the day are still in mind. We teach best when we give ourselves time before class to relax and focus. It helps to take a minimum of half an hour in the office or the empty classroom, going through our lecture plan or quietly sipping a cup of tea, clearing our minds of distraction. Of course we are occasionally affected in class by issues in our personal and professional lives. But our teaching is best when we can concentrate on the work at hand.

In summary, teaching involves the mind because it demands intellectual rigour in content and in process. Teaching involves the heart because it requires empathy, compassion, and respect for our students. Teaching involves the soul because it requires balance, focus, and clarity. Both science and art, teaching is an enterprise that asks us to bring the best of our individual selves to the task.

Course Planning:

Having a Strong Overall Vision

Chapter 4

Setting Out Clear Objectives

I actually get excited about objectives. Even though writing out objectives seems tedious, it brings you back to basics and forces you to think about the very purpose of your teaching. We teach because we think we have something valuable to impart, something specific that we want students to come away with at the end of the semester. Our objectives articulate that. —HR

Objectives can be so invisible in the classroom that it is easy to forget to include them in your planning if you have not received formal teacher-training. Besides, at first glance our instructional objective seems singular: for students to learn the material! But teaching will be more successful if you clarify in your mind what you want students to be able to perform, calculate, think about, analyze, etc., when the course is over. For example, in what specific ways would you like the students to be different after taking your course? Call these ideas "goals" if you like. Whatever term you use, articulating them will prevent you from simply going through the motions of teaching without thinking about what you want students to learn. Your objectives for students should be challenging and specific. They will drive your course and shape your decisions about what material to include and how to teach it.

Most objectives for students will be related to the content of your course, though a few will be cross-disciplinary, for example that students develop a critical approach to evidence or enhance their ability to make academic presentations.

Objectives can roughly be broken into three categories. Are you asking students to acquire knowledge, learn skills, or develop new attitudes? State your objectives in each category.

1. A knowledge objective might suggest:

    •   that students be able to describe relationships between major regions of the human brain;
    •   that students be able to identify underlying causes of the First World War;
    •   that students be able to conjugate irregular French verbs.

2. A skills objective might suggest:

    •   that students be able to apply active-listening techniques in practical occupational-therapy settings;
    •   that students be able to analyze census data in light of sociological theory;
    •   that students be able to use the electron microscope to identify constituents of human cells.

3. An attitudes objective might ask:

    •   that students appreciate the strengths and limitations of the scientific method;
    •   that students develop a taste for 20th Century symphonic music;
    •   that students gain an enthusiasm for statistics.

Your objectives will help you determine what teaching methods to use. If you want students to acquire knowledge, you will lecture, assign readings, ask learners to do outside research and perhaps have them experience each others' class presentations. If you want students to learn skills, you may conduct physical demonstrations and ask class members to attempt and practise those skills. If you want students to develop new attitudes, your teaching style will include discussion to allow individuals to probe their opinions and examine alternative points of view.

So if your goal is that students become familiar with various anthropological definitions of culture, you may discuss several definitions in your lecture and suggest they learn them. Alternatively if you want them to come up with their own views on the different components of culture, you may ensure they have sufficient background information, put them in small groups, give clear instructions, and let them discuss it. If your goal is that students be able to apply a basic math operation to more complex problems, you might teach them the basic principle, make sure they understand it, then give them an application to work on either in class or later. If you want them to learn to analyze corporate balance sheets, you might explain what constitutes analysis, do an analysis yourself while they observe, give them a balance sheet to analyze with a partner, then check their work with the whole group. There are many different choices you can make in the classroom. But generally, what you do in your course depends on your objectives.

Objectives can also be lower-order or higher-order. Cognitively, you may want students merely to describe certain phenomena, or you may have a higher-order hope that they be able to analyze, compare, and critically evaluate new material in the field. Make sure your objectives are realistic based on students' background knowledge and level of sophistication in the discipline. In most situations we ought to strive for a balance of lower and higher objectives. You may want to consult a study of cognitive levels, the best known of which was published almost 50 years ago in Benjamin Bloom's *Taxonomy of Educational Objectives*.[3] From low to high they are:

- knowledge (demonstrating recall or recognition);
- comprehension (understanding, grasping the meaning of, extrapolating from);
- application (showing the use of an idea in concrete situations, applying);
- analysis (breaking material into parts, detecting hierarchies and relationships);
- synthesis (combining to create new patterns and structures);
- evaluation (judging the value of, appraising).

So a lower-order objective might be:

- that students be able to describe and quantify the phenomenon of urbanization in 20th Century India.

A higher-order objective might be:

- that students be able to analyze character motivation in George Eliot's *Middlemarch* in light of political and social upheaval of the period;
- that students evaluate the relative advantages of health-care delivery systems in Canada, Britain, and the United States.

You may also have objectives that apply to you and your teaching. Perhaps you hope to create a supportive environment that will encourage students to express ideas openly. Or you may strive to develop a constructively critical atmosphere that trains students to be discerning when evaluating evidence. Your personal objectives may also include imparting enthusiasm for your discipline, helping students enjoy learning, and encouraging them to develop an increased appreciation for the thoughtful, conscious life. Our objectives help us remember these larger goals.

Chapter 5

Sequencing the Course Material

As the saying goes, you don't really know your discipline until you've taught it. Teaching requires that we have a strong overview, something we rarely achieve as students. Before you teach, then, sit down and take a broad view of the ideas and the information that should be part of the course you are planning. The process helps clarify your own understanding of your field, makes you better able to put information across to others, and allows you to present an integrated and purposeful course.

Keep your large objectives in mind, recalling what you want students to learn. You will need to take into account your established departmental curriculum, especially when you are teaching one of many sections of the same course. In such cases, it is unfair to students if you present only those topics you find most interesting. Nor is it fair to your colleagues who will expect students to possess a prerequisite body of knowledge in later courses. But you will also want to spice up the course with your own special topics of interest and expertise, as well as students' particular interests, which may be different from yours. When introducing extra material, however, be sensitive to colleagues who will teach follow-up courses, by not covering topics that are their purview. In summary, you have duties both to students and to colleagues, to teach material that is an integral part of your course and not emphasize material that rightfully belongs to other courses.

Then, think big and compose a list of topics, themes, ideas, and activities that you might want to include. Appeal to your own professional knowledge and experience. Consult books and resources, but resist drawing an overview straight from the textbook you're going to use. Establish your own ideas before subjecting yourself to the lure of the official resource.

Make sense of the list by adding, subtracting, and grouping like subjects together. The result will be a finite list that will constitute your course. Most courses can be divided into 5 to 10 major topics. For example, an introductory immunology course might break down into: history of the field; antigens and antibodies; cells of the immune system; research methodology; immunodeficiency diseases; autoimmunity; and clinical immunization.

Then, you will need to decide how to break up large topics into sub-topics, and decide on their relative importance. You will decide on time allotments for each, based on the relative importance of each topic and on the amount of information you want to convey. One sub-topic may merit only a mention, while another may deserve an entire class session. You may teach three sub-topics in your Monday class, then devote your entire Wednesday session to a single sub-topic. Draw on your own knowledge of the field when organizing the course material. Your course should be a compromise between your own ideas and what other experts consider important.

You might then decide whether to approach topics and sub-topics as serial or overlapping. Should they be covered in blocks, one after another? Or do one or more particular sub-topics constitute themes that should run through the entire course?

Sequencing

*One reason I enjoyed teaching mathematics is that it's
logical. Each idea builds on the one before. You can't
teach multiplication before teaching addition, because
multiplication is a complex form of addition. The same
is true in learning music and languages. The need for
logical sequencing is not so obvious in some disciplines,
but it's never absent. For example, in a political
philosophy course it would be helpful to discuss Plato
before studying 18th and 19th Century thinkers, many of
whom were responding to Plato's ideas. —HR*

Arranging ideas in a logical sequence constitutes the nuts and bolts
of your course. Does information from Topic B build on that from
Topic A? If so, Topic A should be covered first. Even if you don't
teach a highly sequential discipline such as introductory chemistry
or basic Japanese, you will still need to think about ordering topics
for most effective learning. On what basis should you order the
material? Possibilities include:

1. From the simple to the complex. In biochemistry you might
    choose to discuss unicellular organisms before discussing
    multicellular ones.

2. In chronological order. It often makes sense to introduce events,
    movements, or theories in the order in which they occurred. In
    psychology, one would probably discuss Freud before Jung;
    in physics, Newton's laws of motion before Einstein's theory
    of relativity. History lends itself to a chronological approach
    but can be enhanced by other organizing principles as well.

3. By themes organized around general ideas. For example, a
    course in the history of the 20th Century might include the
    following topics as an alternative to a chronological sequence:
    nationalism; imperialism and war; totalitarianism and
    democracy; populist movements; science and technological

change; mass popular culture; environmental stress; arts and literature; economic change and rise of global enterprise; the transformation of the Third World.

4. According to theoretical models or systems. For example, a course in political economy could be organized around the intellectual models of capitalism, socialism, Keynesian economics, and contemporary globalization. It is sometimes useful to present theories in the form of thesis, antithesis, synthesis, to demonstrate how theoretical approaches developed and changed in reaction to each other.

5. Starting with an idea, a theory, or a phenomenon you personally find compelling. Your enthusiasm may make it a perfect way to initiate a unit of material. From there you can either create webs of interconnected ideas, or move to one of the organizing criteria listed above.

Because no intellectual topic fits neatly into a box, you may decide to combine a number of these approaches. You may want to build into your course a progression from overview to detail and back to overview again. As well, there will usually be ideas that build on a foundation established by other ideas, or that can be understood more easily in reference to those others. Try to arrange your course so that you discuss the foundation ideas first.

It is not necessary that everyone agree with your particular sequencing decisions. There are many legitimate ways to organize a course, and you may present the same material differently from other instructors, based on your professional judgment. But if a colleague asks: "Karen, why did you discuss Kant before you discussed Hegel?" you should be able to give an answer other than "that's the way it is in the book." If it's going to make sense to your students, it must make sense to you. We foster continuity when we start a class with: "Remember that last time we talked about . . . ? Today we're going to take it one step further by discussing . . ."

Organizing and sequencing, vital to preparatory planning, lay the groundwork for detailed scheduling. You can now make up a schedule, complete with specific dates. Factor in special events including quizzes, exams, holidays, guest speakers, labs, practica, or field trips. Then slot in topics and sub-topics according to your organization and sequence. Leave the final class session free of substantive new material; you may need that time to bring closure to a few themes. And you will want time to review and summarize to create a satisfying conclusion to your course.

Courses with Teaching Assistants

If you have teaching assistants (TAs), your planning will include managing them optimally for the best interests of your students, the assistants, and yourself. Depending on your departmental requirements, your TAs may have some built-in responsibilities. For example, your course may be organized as two lectures per week and one small seminar, the latter of which is to be facilitated by a TA. Even so, it will be up to you to outline their responsibilities in total. They should attend all lectures. But how about marking exams, quizzes, and term papers? What percentage of such work should they do? Should you expect your TAs to make up your exams, or contribute questions to them? And should they hold office hours and encourage students to come to them, taking some of the load off you? To decide how much work to assign them, you will need to know how many hours per week each TA has been allotted for your course.

When working with assistants, be clear about your expectations but welcome their suggestions. They are colleagues-in-training, and your work with them should be collaborative. Speak with them frequently, either in regular meetings if that is convenient, or by e-mail or telephone.

We believe it is perfectly fair to your students, and good experience for TAs, for the latter to do some or even most of the grading—as long as you have set the marking criteria and checked to see how each individual will carry them out. Before TAs mark an exam it is important that you review the exam with them, referring to an answer key, so that all markers are agreed on the criteria for what will be considered a poor answer, a fair one, a good one, or an excellent one. Even so, one TA may judge the same work more harshly than would another. Because of that, rather than dividing up the exams among your TAs we recommend making one TA responsible for marking all students' answers to certain particular questions, while another assistant goes through and marks all students' answers to different questions.

It is important to give TAs challenging and interesting work, allowing them to grow professionally from the experience. So, especially if they do not have the opportunity to lead a seminar group, consider encouraging them to give a whole or partial lecture. Our practice has been to give individual TAs (those who want to) an opportunity to make a short presentation (say, 15 minutes of a 50-minute lecture) on a sub-topic in which s/he is particularly interested. If s/he enjoys it and does well, you might suggest the assistant give another, perhaps longer, presentation later in the semester. Obviously this becomes more difficult if you teach a very large class and have a number of assistants.

If your assistants will be leading seminar groups, make it clear what you would like accomplished during the sessions. Should the TAs encourage students to bring questions of clarification from the lecture and from readings? Should the TAs ask students to discuss their opinions about the material? Are the seminars to be practice sessions for skills being learned? Outline for your assistants the basics of leading effective seminars as discussed in Chapter 16. Encourage them to prepare a detailed plan for each session. In these ways you will help them teach as well as possible for the benefit of your students, for the confidence and sense of accomplishment it will give the TAs themselves, and for the integrity of your course.

Chapter 6

The Textbook is Not the Course

Textbooks and supplementary readings exist to support your course, not to drive it. The textbook is not the course. The course is the manifestation of your professional hopes and plans for what your students will learn this semester under your guidance. Sometimes the vision of what your course will be coincides nicely with a textbook. But often your ideas will be somewhat different from those of the text you have been assigned, or the best one you can find.

If you teach a discipline that has access to a large range of excellent textbooks, you may adopt a book that is so good, you'll happily organize your course parallel to it, with Week One discussing Chapter One, Week Two discussing Chapter Two, and so on. If you do, you will still need to plan the delicate balance between textbook topics and outside material. Students rightfully criticize the instructor who only follows the text. Even if you are working with the perfect book, to challenge students as well as yourself it is important that you bring in fresh examples, different theories or points of view, and the occasional relevant item from yesterday's newspaper. You will also provide the overview, examples, connections among ideas, and clarification of difficult concepts that are sometimes lacking in textbooks.

Once we have adopted certain textbooks and readings, it is easy to feel like slaves to them. Instead, we should assign readings that make sense given what we want to accomplish. Omit articles, chapters, or pages that are irrelevant or simply too much material for your course. Don't be afraid to take chapters out of order. Assign readings in a sequence that facilitates the flow, vision, and objectives of your course. You might, for example, want to emphasize a sub-topic that is one of your own areas of research or special interest, or one that you think will be engaging to this particular group of students. No matter how a topic is treated in the textbook, deal with it as you see fit. However, remember that if you alter the order of textbook topics you may need to fill in background information. Design your course in a way that touches on all necessary topics but allows you to speak enthusiastically and knowledgably given your particular passions and expertise.

If you're teaching one of the umpteen sections of a standardized introductory or survey course, you may be required to ask your students to read the entire textbook. That's fine. You can still put your vigorous individual stamp on the course by emphasizing those chapters you think are important. If you're teaching an idiosyncratic course of your own design or, say, Genetics for Arts Students, you can assign what readings you choose because students will not proceed on to more advanced courses in the discipline.

Plan to give students guidance when asking them to read Chapter 4 or Article B. Especially for first- or second-year students, direct them to specific questions to consider during their reading. These can be as simple as: "What is the author's thesis, and what evidence does she marshal to support it?" Or it could be more specific: "This article discusses Malinowski's observations among Trobriand Islanders. After reading the article, summarize three such observations, and think about them in relation to Margaret Mead's work in Samoa that we discussed last week." You will also seek a range of students' responses to the readings, and encourage their creative analysis. But some initial questions give them direction, and turn intangible assignments into tangible ones.

Many instructors want students to gain experience with a variety of sources, and therefore assign outside readings along with a textbook. Such materials should be relevant, interesting, and at an appropriate level of complexity. Some instructors deliver a 3-ring binder to the reserve desk of the campus library and regularly insert articles that students can borrow and copy. However, students sometimes take articles from the binder and fail to return them because the students are in a hurry, because they don't have money for the photocopier, or because returning the articles is otherwise inconvenient. Furthermore, when students are competing against each other for grades, they may occasionally sabotage each other's efforts by stealing articles so others will not have access. If you put reading materials on reserve, check with students to make sure the system is working. Alternatively, you can make up a readings package of articles and other materials that students purchase from the bookstore at the start of term. This is a good method for ensuring that all students receive specific articles, chapters, and other materials that you would like to include, such as lecture outlines.

You will occasionally teach with a textbook you dislike. If this is because you could not find a better book, it is acceptable to tell students the textbook has limitations and you're sorry nothing better was available. They'll understand. However, don't ask them to spend $100 on a textbook, then spend the rest of the semester telling them how mediocre it is.

If the textbook you dislike was chosen by colleagues, best not to give students your unexpurgated opinion, which might be perceived as criticism of co-workers. However, it is always acceptable to offer your opinion of a textbook's strengths and weaknesses, and to introduce supplementary readings. You can even turn an experience with a poor textbook into a useful intellectual exercise by asking students to suggest ways in which the book could be improved.

When the textbook isn't ideal I like to tell students:
"Maybe one of you will some day write a really excellent
textbook on this topic." I'm serious. One of my best

*undergraduate instructors used to say: "Medical re-
searchers don't yet understand why such-and-such, but
who knows? Maybe someone right here in this room will
find out."[4] When I was a student, it sent chills down my
spine. —EB*

Chapter 7

Helping Students with Thinking and Writing

T his book is about the process of instruction, not the content. But there are two content-related issues—thinking and writing—that cut across disciplines and are important no matter what subject we teach. Many books have been written on these topics, which we will not address extensively here. Instead we will make a few general comments.

Critical Thinking

When I was an undergraduate, I thought that learning consisted of opening books and reading facts that other people had laid out. I didn't really understand that learning is about assessing evidence from different sources, each of which has an implicit point of view.
—HR

Critical thinking is a set of habits, tendencies, attitudes, skills, and strategies regarding knowledge that we seek to pass along to our students. In doing so we can help them go beyond memorization of facts to evaluation of information, and bring an educated and considered approach to data, theories, and ideas.

A critical-thinking approach possesses characteristics that we should model for our students. It is open-minded without being gullible. It is analytical, making comparisons and distinctions. It asks that any experts who are being cited are legitimate and credible authorities in the field. When looking at evidence for an inference or a conclusion, it demands that the evidence be relevant, acceptable, and sufficient.[5] According to one useful document on the topic, the critical thinker is habitually inquisitive, well informed, trustful of reason, flexible, fair-minded in evaluation, honest in facing personal biases, and willing to reconsider.[6]

We want our students to realize that all evidence contains points of view. Whether you and your students are discussing priorities in cancer research or the merits of bank mergers, you can encourage learners to critically examine sources of information. As the historian Paul Thompson succinctly puts it, the general rules in examining evidence are to look for internal consistency, to seek confirmation in other sources, and to be aware of potential bias.[7] Looking for internal consistency means analyzing whether evidence is logical and plausible without any obvious anomalies. Seeking confirmation in other sources (sometimes called external consistency) means checking several sources to see whether they agree. Being aware of potential bias requires that we look for factors that may have influenced a writer's point of view. Could the author have profited in any way from promoting a given viewpoint? Does the author have a strong ideological position that might affect his argument? Was the author's writing affected by her time and place, her cultural background, or her academic discipline and particular lens through which she views the controversy? Many factors go into shaping an author's beliefs and attitudes. We want to coach students to identify those points of view. In this quest we may also be reminded of our own biases and preconceptions.

We can help our students develop critical-thinking qualities. The most basic exercise is to have students practise stating in one or two sentences the main thesis or main idea of a piece of writing. This can be extended by asking them to identify aspects of the author's point of view. We can also give students exercises in developing inferences from incomplete information such as newspaper articles, conversations, or pamphlets. Or we can have them compare and evaluate several sources on the same topic. Ideally, the goal is to teach our students to develop a critical attitude toward the information they encounter, the sources they consult, and the evidence they analyze.

Writing

Writing skills constitute another cross-disciplinary educational issue. Closely tied to thinking itself, effective writing encourages clear thinking and vice versa.

Most instructors would agree that writing ability is a basic component of education, and that competent communication should be expected from university students. People need to learn to express their ideas if they are to be successful in any academic discipline or future line of work. On the other hand, stringent writing requirements penalize students who have only been working in the English language for a few months or years. They may also penalize an entire generation that had easier access to television than to books. Furthermore, our contract with students is usually to teach them cultural anthropology or physics, not English composition. For most of us writing is not our expertise. And to top it off, we don't have time.

However, if writing is valuable, we suggest that there are ways in which we can help students develop in this regard, without taking much class time. First, tell students that you consider good writing important. Second, require that they write, and give them resources to help. These can include a few basic books you put on reserve at the library, or directions to your college's writing support centre. Third, consider outlining for students—during a brief discussion in class or in a handout—a few central qualities of good writing.

We suggest you point out to students that there are two basic objectives in good writing: (1) making the work clear, and (2) making it interesting.

1. Making the work clear.

    (a) Writing is clearest when it is concise. Encourage your students, when editing their own work, to remove unnecessary words and phrases. Reducing a passage to the basics usually indicates whether the idea has been expressed comprehensibly. Emphasize that longer papers will not necessarily receive better marks than short ones; consider stipulating that writing assignments be concise, for example, no more than two pages.

    All of us occasionally use unnecessary words to equivocate or to pad our writing. Sentences are clearer without such words. Teach your students to recognize and remove phrases such as: "it is usually the case that," "at this point in time," "in regard to," "in terms of," "it appears that," "has a tendency to," "the concept of," "the process of," and "it should be noted that." Edit out unnecessary phrases starting with "that," "which," and "who." For example, "the people who are located in" can be shortened to "the people in"; similarly, "the tasks that are involved in" is better expressed as "the tasks in . . ."[8]

    (b) Ambiguous pronoun reference is one of the most common impediments to clear writing. This problem arises when it is not obvious which noun is referred to by a pronoun such as "that," "their," or "he." Teach your students to check each pronoun reference, using the following general rules. Keep the pronoun as close to the noun as possible. Do not use a pronoun before the noun has been introduced. When a pronoun could refer to several nouns in the same sentence, repeat the noun rather than using the pronoun.

    (c) Parallel constructions (verb tense, singular versus plural, noun versus verb form) in a list of words or a series of phrases help make the meaning clear and prevent a reader from having to go back and re-read the sentence.

2. Making the work interesting.

   (a) Use the active rather than the passive voice, to make writing more dynamic.

   (b) Vary sentence length and structure to add stimulus and diversity to the work. Rather than always writing subject-verb-object, from time to time begin a sentence with an introductory phrase or clause. Occasionally use short sentences.

   (c) Employ strong verbs rather than relying solely on adjectives and adverbs. Choosing the most precise or interesting verb avoids unnecessary modifiers and makes writing more lively. You can demonstrate this point graphically by having students brainstorm, either as a whole class or in small groups, how many synonyms they can think of for the word "speak" or "run," or how many verbs they can think of to describe human movement.

To remind yourself of writing principles, and to introduce these principles to your students, there are few better references than the classic little book *The Elements of Style*.[9]

You may want to give students short writing assignments in which it is feasible for you to address writing beyond just circling punctuation and spelling mistakes. "Please write a one-page paper summarizing the main ideas from today's lecture. Half of the 5-point mark for the paper will be assessed on the quality of your writing." (For more on evaluating writing assignments, see Chapter 35.) If you don't have time to give such assignments, simply stating that you value and reward good writing will encourage students to develop this important ability, which will also help them become clearer thinkers and well-rounded learners.

Chapter 8

Designing Assignments and Term Projects

A ssignments offer a world of possibilities, both for yourself and for your students. Distinct from examinations, they should offer something apart from what exams do. They provide an opportunity for students to investigate topics in depth, to conduct independent research, and to practise writing or other skills. In addition, assignments are important as a different means of evaluation—especially useful for students who tend not to perform well on exams due to test anxiety or their particular learning styles, and who need time to think out their ideas. Assignments also appeal to students who have analytical or organizational skills that may not be evident on examinations.

Most college and university assignments come in the form of written essays, usually based on reading, research, and reasoning: "For your first assignment, please write an 8-page, 2500-word paper analyzing one of the novels of Dostoyevsky or Tolstoy in its social and political context." Such standard essay assignments have an important place in learning, but are only one of many possible assignment types. There are a number of steps you can take to ensure that research projects of all kinds provide a valuable learning experience for your students.

Projects should be specific enough to give direction and not call for expertise the students don't possess. Most projects you assign should give students clear guidelines regarding the proposed topic, how they might go about researching it, and how they might present it in final form. You can also help students by suggesting that they follow a series of steps: find a topic, then gather sources, then craft an outline, then write a draft, then rewrite.[10]

> *In my first year of teaching I was excited and wanted students to be working on projects that excited them. I asked students to think about the huge range of topics in the course, choose any one, and design a research project to investigate any facet of that topic. They should see it as an opportunity to delve into a question that fascinated them. And they should come see me during office hours if they needed help. Well, for weeks until the paper was due, there was a lineup of students at my office, desperately needing guidance. Aside from lacking the methodological tools, most of them were drowning in a sea of infinite possible topics. I've never assigned such an open-ended project again. —EB*

Assignments should be designed to minimize potential plagiarism, a large problem in post-secondary education today. (See Chapter 36.) The most familiar type of plagiarism is that in which students use ideas or words without attribution, either from lack of understanding of academic standards or because they think they can get away with it. An increasingly widespread type of plagiarism, though, involves the straight-out purchasing of papers from professional writers or essay-hoarders. Only a minority of students would stoop to this practice, but it does occur. We therefore favour assignments that are specific to the students' experience or class-work. So you might consider: "For the next assignment, I'd like you to write a paper of approximately 500 words. The paper should take the main principles of today's lecture on world food supply, and use those principles to explain data from the *Science* journal article that I put on hold for you in the library." That kind of assignment is difficult to purchase, and has the additional advantage of requiring students to understand and apply information from your lecture.

To ensure that students really have learned from a research project, you might consider requiring that they write summary papers in class, with no notes. This obviously requires that they learn the material well beforehand. One disadvantage, however, is that their papers will be unlikely to include the amount of attribution you would normally expect in university-level academic work. Try to keep in-class papers short, to save class time and to minimize the amount of hand-written work you are compelled to decipher.

Be cautious about asking students to write position papers on topics you feel strongly about, for example: Should alcohol and cigarette companies be further restricted in how they advertise? Should the legal system treat aboriginal offenders differently from non-aboriginal ones? Should regulations be tightened on the use of animals in research? Should society permit the production of genetically modified foods? Whatever the issue, if you feel passionately about it, you may have difficulty grading papers in an unbiased manner and assessing them purely on academic grounds. If you want students to tackle controversial issues, one approach is to ask them to argue both pros and cons, and grade students on the strength of their research and thought rather than on the particular positions taken.

When assigning projects we sometimes offer open-ended alternatives, by telling students that if any of them has an original project idea, s/he is welcome to come to the office and discuss it. If you try this, the number of students you receive at your office will depend on how enthusiastically you present this option. We suggest you not over-encourage it for first-year undergraduates, who sometimes lack the skills to work independently. As students mature in their education, they become more able to initiate and follow through on original ideas. Even in graduate school, though, students can use the gentle guidance of an experienced professor.

Innovative Assignments

Students can be inspired by creative and non-traditional assignments. When we were undergraduates, one memorable Sociology project required that students sit on benches in various neighbourhoods and observe aspects of people's lives, using course theory to make sense of their observations.[11] Another assignment asked students to attend a religious service of a tradition different from their own, and write about it. Among other projects, we as instructors have assigned students to: (a) attend a concert of an unfamiliar musical genre and analyze it—demonstrating an understanding of music theory; and (b) practise communication skills with friends, keeping a diary of successes and problems. We suggest you use your imagination and think expansively when developing assignments.

A variety of assignment types helps accommodate students' different learning styles and different kinds of intelligence—some organizational, some creative, some analytical. Non-traditional assignments also provide balance and interest for your course, and can make it more personally meaningful to students. Instead of requiring three written papers, consider requiring two papers plus one other assignment that might be a presentation, a debate, a demonstration, a discussion-facilitation, or a group project. You might ask students to conduct interviews for an oral-history paper on local geography or politics. Perhaps you would like to take a risk and allow students to make videos or multimedia projects. One of our colleagues has students conduct research projects and present the information in poster sessions at the end of the semester, as if at an academic conference.[12]

There are other alternatives to typical research and term-paper assignments, including novel ways to encourage students to improve their writing. Here are a few valuable assignment ideas from *Tools for Teaching* by Barbara Gross Davis.[13]

- abstract for an academic journal, in which you give students a published article with the abstract removed;

- book review or article, written as if for a professional journal;
- letter to an editor or a public official. Students each write a persuasive letter, presenting evidence and responding to arguments;
- invented dialogue, written as if two individuals were discussing an issue.

How Many Assignments?

How many assignments should you expect students to complete in a term? In a typical quarter or semester lasting 10 to 14 weeks, you may give (along with several exams) as few as one substantive assignment or as many as ten or more short ones which may be exercise sets, short papers, or lab write-ups. Discuss with your colleagues what is a reasonable number to assign. Bear in mind your desire to give students variety so they can develop and realize their diverse strengths and learning styles. But also consider how busy the students are, especially if they are in professional programs and taking many other courses concurrently.

Another important consideration when planning assignments is the amount of time they will take you to grade. Enthusiasm can sometimes lead instructors to assign projects that later consume heroic numbers of grading hours. Say your term projects are sufficiently complex that each student's submission will require an hour to grade. If there are 40 students in the class, the arithmetic is simple. Where will you, or even your teaching assistants, find 40 hours near the end of term, what with organizing exams, planning final lectures, and attending to other professional responsibilities, not to mention attempting to maintain personal lives?

We have discovered that some of the most interesting and pedagogically sound projects can also be graded fairly quickly. But they must be designed carefully. We suggest short papers, which are quicker to grade than long ones but are equally good learning experiences. In fact, some instructors argue that short papers require more-disciplined writing on the part of the student, and are therefore pedagogically superior. We also suggest assignments that are amenable to being graded with the aid of a check-list or criteria-sheet, so that you can read the paper speedily looking for required elements A, B, and C. This will not only streamline your grading but make it more accurate and fair. (See Chapter 35.) No matter what kinds of assignments you design, whether traditional or non-traditional, written or otherwise, think out the specifics of how you will evaluate students and let them know in advance. The more precise your grading criteria, the fewer arguments you will get from students and the more confident you will be in the fairness of your system.

Chapter 9

Producing a Course Outline or Syllabus

The handouts that you distribute on the first day of class should be necessary orienteering maps for your students through the landscape of your course. Spend time ensuring that such handouts are organized, specific, accurate, and complete. Writing a comprehensive syllabus forces you to think out your policies, of which there are dozens to consider. How will you deal with students who miss exams? How about that slippery issue of participation: if you plan to reward it, how will you assess it? On written papers, how many marks will you deduct for poor grammar and spelling, or assign to the more subjective issue of writing style? On exams, will you accept any written answer you can decipher and mark purely on intellectual content, or will you downgrade a good answer that is barely legible or badly articulated? Then you need policies for formatting of papers, for missed deadlines, and for assignment expectations. All such issues should be thought out before the semester and, ideally, listed on your syllabus. Composing a comprehensive syllabus also saves you copious time throughout the semester, time that you would otherwise spend repeatedly telling students: "My policy on make-up exams is . . ." or: "Your Internet sources should meet the following criteria . . ." All of this should be on your course outline or syllabus. A comprehensive syllabus will make you and your students feel organized and confident, and will save you effort and frustration throughout the term. Encourage students to bring the syllabus to class by letting them know you will refer to it often.

Let's say you distribute one main handout that you call your Course Outline. It should contain:

1. The what, when, and where of the course. Course number and title (ENGL 100: Introduction to English Literature). Location of classes. Days, times, and duration of classes.

2. The who of the course—in this case, you. Your full name (and, if you like, what you prefer to be called). Office location and hours, office phone number, e-mail address. A little information about yourself as it is relevant to the course. Some instructors include their home phone numbers. Others prefer not to do so, but keep in close touch with their office voice mail and e-mail to be able to answer student questions quickly.

3. A grading profile. A description of exams and assignments, with percentage marks for each one, totalling 100%. Institutional or course policies on what constitutes A, B, C, D and F work, or, in Pass-Fail courses, a Pass.

4. Dates for all exams and quizzes. Due-dates for assignments.

5. Explanations of assignments in enough detail that students could accomplish the work without further discussion with you. That is not to say you won't speak about assignments in class. But include all important elements on the handout. That means a description of the assignment and how many marks it is worth, and details on research policies and expectations. For written assignments you might say how long papers should be, in what style they should be written, and the degree to which quality of writing will be factored into grading.

6. Your expectations of students. This can include basic rules of conduct and respect, especially in courses dealing with

controversial topics. It can say whether class attendance is mandatory. It can also include reminders of students' responsibility for their learning and for the grades they earn.

7. A variety of policy matters. For example, you may accept only word-processed or typewritten, rather than handwritten, papers. If you give marks for participation, spell out your criteria. (See Chapter 33.)

8. Policies concerning late papers and make-up examinations. We recommend that such policies be rigorous but allow for occasional leniency. Some instructors do not mention late papers and make-ups on the course outline, believing that to do so might demonstrate low expectations. We feel differently about it. Students have complicated lives just as we do, and from time to time genuinely cannot meet deadlines. If you do not address this issue on your course outline, you may end up verbally explaining the policy numerous times and having some students misunderstand it. Better to save your energy for important discussions, and publish the rules up-front. Regarding exams, you might decide to allow make-ups for major exams when the student has spoken to you beforehand and has a serious reason for missing the scheduled exam. If you give a number of shorter tests or quizzes, consider a system in which you do not allow make-ups (which are time-consuming for you to organize and monitor). Instead you might give five small quizzes throughout the semester; no make-ups allowed for missed quizzes, but only students' best four quizzes will count, which allows them to miss one. Although we support such a policy for small quizzes, we caution that this type of "best-two-out-of-three" system can become onerous for you with major exams that take abundant time and effort to grade. You may regret spending hours marking exams that then don't count toward students' grades.

9. A schedule, complete with topics to be covered and readings that students should have finished before each session. Some

instructors prefer the flexibility of a loose schedule in which they simply list topics to be covered during the semester, not tied to particular dates. As fans of structure—flexible structure, but structure nonetheless—we recommend against loose scheduling. If you do not stick to a prearranged timetable—for example of one major topic per week—by halfway through the course you may be lagging with no possible way to cover the planned material. You may have to scramble to reorganize, and eliminate or give short shrift to major topics. Students will not be impressed by your organizational skills, and will be disadvantaged by your skipping major topics if they plan to take follow-up courses in the discipline. To avoid unpleasantness, make up a schedule and do your best to adhere to it. If, during the semester, you have to make slight alterations, simply make an announcement in class. Most students prefer a change in schedule to no schedule at all.

The schedule can be presented either class-by-class or week-by-week. The first option has the advantage of letting students know exactly what they should read for each individual session. The second option provides a little more leeway but is still organized enough to keep you on schedule and make students feel secure.

Jan 5	Session 1	Historical and social roots of impressionist art
Jan 7	Session 2	Characteristics and influence of impressionism
Jan 12	Session 3	Monet and other impressionist artists
Jan 14	Session 4	Later artists who were influenced by impressionism

or:

| Jan 5–7 | Week 1 | Roots of impressionism; characteristics of the art |
| Jan 12–14 | Week 2 | Impressionist and post-impressionist artists |

Once you have distributed your course outline, urge students to read it carefully. Review it in the first class. (See Chapter 12.) If students read the handout and then still have questions, these should be welcomed. Sometimes students' questions demonstrate a weakness in the course outline in which a point may be unclear or information may have been omitted inadvertently. Sometimes students' queries demonstrate their main areas of concern or insecurity, which are good for you to know.

If you are distributing more than one handout, consider making each one a different colour, so you can talk students through a handout by directing them clearly to it, saying: "As you will see on the yellow sheet, second paragraph . . ." However, if you teach numerous courses per semester, you may want to try a different system. To avoid losing or confusing papers from various courses, we assign a particular colour to all papers for any given course. So there's "the blue course" and "the yellow course," or "the pink course" and "the green course." Any handouts that are generic to more than one course are simply white. But any handouts or quizzes that are specifically for, say, the blue course, are printed up in blue. For us, it cuts down on the nasty habit of placing papers in wrong file folders, not to be found again until it's too late.

Class Planning:

Being Thoroughly Organized for Each Session

Chapter 10

Organizing Day-to-Day Teaching

Planning for each individual class is much of the moment-to-moment reality of being an instructor. Every Friday you know that come Monday morning you will be standing in front of a group of people looking to you to provide leadership, impart information, direct them to resources, and inspire learning. It's a daunting task to take on several times a week and sometimes several times a day. So how do you plan class sessions to be as successful, and to accomplish as many of your objectives, as possible? What will you do with your students for 50 minutes or more?

Lecturing, the most familiar teaching strategy in higher education, will probably form a significant component of your class activities. Though somewhat unfashionable given the current emphasis on student-centred and cooperative learning, lecturing remains extremely valuable if done well. Lectures serve specific purposes including dissemination of information, explanation of concepts, clarification of readings, and identification of connections and context. They provide a personal touch to learning that students cannot obtain from the textbook or a web-site. In addition, lectures can be engaging and interactive, so that students are involved throughout.

Good lectures are well-organized. In planning a lecture, sit down with some blank paper and the textbook, readings, or other resources. It may help to make a list of ideas you consider important on the topic. You may have to do some extra reading to freshen up on sub-topics. It is important to finalize your ideas in an outline. Depending on how familiar you are with the subject matter, make notes for yourself, either general or more detailed. Outline the information into a few main sections and sub-sections. Prepare to introduce the lecture by letting students know what it's going to be about, and why the topic is relevant or important. Good lectures also contain effective examples, stories, and other elements to bring the information alive and make it memorable. The best lecturers frequently summarize to let listeners know where the lecture has been, where it is now, and where it is going.

Of course we should have sufficient material prepared for each class session. But like a cook who invites half a dozen friends over for dinner and prepares enough food for 20, most instructors plan more material for a given class session than they can or should use. Understandable as this tendency may be, it sometimes causes us to rush through classes, implying that questions would be an imposition and anesthetizing students so they become unable to do anything other than scribble.

Use your professional judgment to determine how much detail is necessary at your particular course level, and try not to overload students with too much. After all, part of an instructor's job is to help students assess and discriminate. When a small amount of information is good, that doesn't mean more will be better.

Variety and Participation

Along with periods of lecturing, you will probably want to provide variety and opportunities for student participation. Variety is desirable because people have limited attention spans for unchanging stimuli. We may lament that a so-called television generation demands entertainment in their education today, but much of students' need for diverse activities is natural. We can achieve variety in our classes in many ways, from showing a video, to giving a demonstration, to asking students to fill out a survey for discussion.

Students learn most, and enjoy it most, when they engage with the material. Participation can be elicited in a number of ways, the most familiar of which is to ask the entire class a question about the academic material. When using this technique, note that some kinds of questions spark useful discussion, while others do not. (See Chapter 22.) As well, consider alternatives to whole-group discussion. There are numerous participatory strategies, including various kinds of small-group work and writing exercises that you can introduce, modify, refine, and make your own. (See Chapter 13.)

Many instructors are reluctant to encourage participation because of a felt obligation to "cover the material." But as we all know, that's an impossible task. Given the few dozen hours we have with our students in a given course per semester, we simply cannot exhaust all the material of interest or importance to our field. Besides, considering the excellent textbooks, Internet, and other resources available, imparting information is no longer our only task as educators. We need to provide students with perspective on the field, elaborate on how ideas relate to each other, and help students learn to discern the more-important from the less-important. We also help students organize new material, provide a forum for discussion, explain concepts that are particularly difficult or compelling, assist students to think clearly and critically, and motivate them to go out and do the reading and other work that will teach them the majority of what they will learn in our field. Ideally, teaching is not only informational, but inspirational.

An effective class provides students with a reasonable amount of new or challenging information, but also involves them continually with the material. When planning, build in frequent opportunities for genuine and widespread participation. This will help students learn more, and give them brief breaks from continuous lecture.

We strongly suggest you not leave student involvement until the end of every class session. Students will more readily take part if you punctuate classes with frequent opportunities for participation. If you lecture non-stop for 45 minutes of a 50-minute class, then ask students to discuss the material, they won't. There are several reasons:

- Discussion is more lively and meaningful when material is discussed immediately. A few minutes later, students have lost the excitement of the moment.
- The amount of material raised in 45 minutes is too much to discuss all at once. They're overwhelmed.
- Students have become comfortable in a passive role.
- The clock is ticking. They're beginning to worry about their next class or commitment and can't give your question the energy it requires.

Structuring Sessions

There are many ways to organize a class. Here is one basic model, in which information and ideas can be presented as introduction, lecture, student activity, and evaluation. First you introduce the topic, then impart information on it, then give students an involving exercise in which to apply or otherwise understand the information. At some point, immediately or later, you evaluate students on their learning and yourself on your teaching. It's a useful model that can be adapted to many needs and situations.

1. An effective introduction or warm-up might be an evocative story, a verbal reference to a recent news item relating to the topic at hand, or a question on the overhead that stimulates student thinking. It may simply put students in the mood for learning. A review of previously-taught information and skills can also provide a useful introduction to a session. It could be as simple as asking if there are any questions about last day's class. We keep review snappy to avoid belabouring

points. You can throw out quick questions. "Remember that we talked about two ways to do such-and-such. What was one of those?" . . . "What was the other?"

2. The lecture is our imparting of information. It can be short or long, but should be well-organized and enthusiastically presented. The lecture can be interspersed with questions and exercises, so that lecture and activity are not mutually exclusive.

3. The activity can be anything from class discussion to group work to individual work on problem-sets. It is a good idea to develop a small repertoire of participatory activities to provide interest and address various academic needs.

4. Evaluation can be done frequently or infrequently, with formal tests and quizzes or in other forms. You can ask quick questions for students to self-test. You can assign problems for students to discuss in pairs. You can ask students to summarize points or answer questions on paper. You can even check notebooks. There are many methods by which you and your students can get a sense of whether the teaching has met its objectives and whether learning has taken place. Periodic review goes hand-in-hand with ongoing evaluation. Not all evaluation has to be for marks.

In summary, the best classes have an ordered mix of lecture and activities that provide momentum and energy, and allow students to be involved. The next chapter will suggest how to effectively translate your ideas into minute-by-minute planning for the classroom.

Chapter 11

Writing Step-by-Step Lecture Plans

You may know a few of those unusual professors who walk into class with no notes and speak eloquently for 50 minutes. Their extraordinary minds and natural flair for public speaking make them legendary. For the rest of us, however, lecture plans are a must.

A lecture plan is the step-by-step outline that you create for yourself and carry into the classroom, detailing just about everything you are going to do in a given class session. School-teachers call them lesson plans. If your teaching style minimizes straight lecturing, you could call them class plans or session plans. Whether or not you use lecture as your main teaching strategy, we'll call this outline a lecture plan. Whatever you label it, it is necessary for your effectiveness in the classroom and your enjoyment of the work.

"Should I illustrate this concept using Example A or Example B?" "Is Theory X important enough to include in today's lecture?" "Should I put students into small groups to discuss this, or take comments from the class as a whole?" "How should I word the question to kick off the discussion most effectively?" Every class session requires dozens of small decisions. Think out as many as possible before class, and write instructions to yourself as part of the plan.

A lecture plan helps you feel organized and minimizes the number of important decisions you must make on the spot. It allows you to concentrate on the immediate aspects of teaching—conveying the intellectual content, keeping your presentation varied and interesting, monitoring student reactions, and asking and answering questions well—by liberating you from worrying about mechanics.

You will have your plan on the desk or lectern in front of you, and refer to it often throughout the session. It should be reasonably detailed, but not so detailed that you will get lost looking at it or be forced to keep your finger on it to retain your place. It should order your ideas clearly and logically, in easy-to-read outline format, as you will present them. It should contain:

1. How you will start the session. A note on what story, question, reminder, or review you will use to begin.

2. The progression of ideas, from start to finish, with 5- to 15-minute time allotments for each section. This can be done in standard outline form with large headings denoting the three or four main sections of your lecture, with sub-headings underneath, and sub-sub-headings if necessary.

3. Examples you will use. Don't leave it until the last minute to decide which anecdote would best illustrate Cold War tensions between the United States and the Soviet Union, or the influence of postmodernism on media. Decide beforehand, and jot down a reminder on your outline.

4. Questions you will ask students. If you feel it would be stimulating at a certain point in the lecture to have students list similarities and differences between Hinduism and Buddhism, or causes of worldwide deterioration of coral reefs, make a note to yourself. Many's the time we have let the "questionable" moment slip by, never to be recaptured.

5. Any instructions you are going to give, complete with wording for maximum clarity. So, for example, you may plan to say the following about a term paper: "Students, remember there is no need for a cover page—let's save a tree on this one. Second, please double-space. Third, your paper should not be over five pages in length. Fourth, have it ready to hand in at the beginning of class next Tuesday." On your lecture plan, you would list the instructions clearly in point form: (a) no cover page, (b) double-spaced, (c) five pages maximum, (d) due next Tuesday.

6. Ideas for transitions between topics. A transition can be as simple as: "Those were South African socioeconomic conditions under apartheid. Now, let's talk about conditions in that country after apartheid." Or the transition can be more complex or subtle. The point is, you should always be ready with your next topic, and not be forced to pause for inordinate amounts of time to collect your thoughts.

7. Plans for discussions or small-group work. Where you anticipate an opportunity for student input or debate, do not just write "discussion" and assume it will take care of itself. Jot down the mechanics if there are any (for example, of organizing students into groups), the questions you will raise, and the points you hope will be brought out.

8. Logistical details. If you will be handing out paper at some point, think beforehand about how best to accomplish that. Should the paper be available for students to pick up on the way into the room? Should you or your teaching assistants hand it out partway through class? How can you expedite such proceedings to take a minimum of time and trouble? If you're using a video, you will have cued it up before class and ensured that the TV/VCR is functioning. But what if you have several machines to coordinate partway through class? Think ahead and give yourself brief written reminders on how to get things done efficiently.

9. Housekeeping items. You may need to remind students of exams, future events, or administrative requirements. Make sure to list all these reminders. This will help you avoid the embarrassing end-of-class moment, which we've all experienced, of students pulling on their coats and scrambling out of the room as we attempt to regain their attention with information on next week's assignment. As well, think about when to address such items. Many instructors get them out of the way at the start of class. This is preferable to dealing with them in the last few minutes, which produces a weak ending to the session. However, you may also want to add a brief reminder of a quiz or guest speaker as you are wrapping up at the end of class. Other options for addressing housekeeping items include after a break in a long class, or sandwiched as a mental break between major sections of content.

10. How you will conclude. You might tie things together by referring to an idea from the start of the session, you might simply summarize your main points, or you might want to foreshadow classes to come. You may want to wrap up the session with a thought-provoking point arising from the day's discussions. Whatever you decide, bring the class to an energetic and spirited conclusion.

A sample outline for a lecture plan

A. Introduction   10:00
   1. Brief story illustrating theme of today's class
   2. Circulate handout
   3. "Any questions from last session?"

B. Announcements   10:05
   1. Reminder about quiz on Wednesday
   2. Guest speaker coming next month

C. Lecture: Major topic   10:10
  1. Background to topic
     a. Its history
     b. Its influence
     c. Specific examples of its application
  2. Expand on topic
     a. . . .
     b. . . .
  3. Question to students: 10:20
     "(precise wording of question)"
     Discussion with class as a whole.

D. Small-group work   10:25
  1. Procedural instructions for group work
     a. first instruction
     b. second instruction
  2. Students form groups, discuss for 5 minutes
  3. Get students' attention; debrief with class
  4. Summarize main points of group discussions

E. Lecture: Second major topic   10:35
  1. Sub-topic
  2. Relation to other topics

F. Wrap-up, conclusion   10:45
  1. Summary of points. Why are these issues
     important?
  2. Question to consider for next class
  3. Any last reminders.
     "Thanks, everybody. See you next time."   10:49

Writing the Plan

All instructors have their own personal styles. Different situations, too, may call for different kinds of lecture plans. In some cases you may want an abbreviated lecture plan along with extensive notes on separate sheets of paper. In other cases you might want a more detailed outline.

An abbreviated sample plan appears on the following page. It has less detail than we would normally include, but illustrates an effective organizational format.

The fact that you have a lecture plan does not mean you won't be open to the spontaneous. A preplanned structure will not prevent useful digressions. Occasionally a student will raise an unforeseen issue providing, as the saying goes, a teachable moment. Seize the opportunity. Make the point(s), then go back to your outline. Not only will a good lecture plan allow you the occasional digression, it may actually facilitate it. Like a personal budget that allows you to know how much money you possess, therefore whether you can afford a small spontaneous purchase, so a good lecture plan allows you to know exactly where you are in a session and whether you can afford the luxury of discussing a tangential but interesting question. It occasionally happens that a spontaneous student discussion is so energizing and illuminating that you should be prepared to adjust your plan substantially. You do not want to feel limited by your lecture plan, which should serve your purposes rather than vice versa. On the other hand, sessions are usually most productive when you follow your well-thought-out plan.

While planning your class, it can be helpful to mentally rehearse your lecture plan. As you rehearse you may want to stand, rather than sit, in your office for enhanced reality testing. Think of a playwright who speaks the words aloud as s/he is writing them, to make sure the dialogue will flow and have the intended effect when spoken on stage. Imagine yourself in the classroom delivering the material. Does it have an interesting or upbeat beginning? Do the ideas flow in some intentional sequence? Are the examples up-to-date and compelling? How's the timing? How will you wrap up the class in a way that emphasizes important points and provides closure?

We cannot over-emphasize the value of deliberately writing the lecture plan. Whether you write it with your computer or your pen, the process of mentally walking through the class step-by-step will clarify your thinking, produce a logical sequence of information and activities, and remind you of details (either content or form) you may otherwise forget. Lecture plans are so important to effective instruction that teachers-in-training for the school system spend many hours learning how to design them, having their plans critiqued, then reworking them.

Your lecture plan should indicate roughly how much time you will spend on each section. We suggest you write "15 minutes" or "10:15–10:30" right on your plan. Before a 50-minute class, if your preparation suggests that you have 90 minutes of material, resist saying to yourself: "I'd rather have too much than too little. It'll work out." Preparing too much material is a natural reaction to the terrifying thought of running out of things to say halfway through the session. But, as part of your planning, decide—in advance—and indicate on your lecture outline which section(s) you will leave out if the class is running short of time. Then, if a particular discussion runs longer than you expected, you can eliminate a pre-chosen section of the lecture effortlessly without having to mentally reorganize on the spot.

What's wrong with just preparing a large amount of material and getting through as much as you can in a given class? University lecturers commonly proceed in this manner, and your students are unlikely to complain. But if you want to turn a good class into a great one, plan for it to be an integrated whole with a beginning, a middle, and an end, like a carefully crafted term paper or an artful work of literature.

Chapter 12

The First Class Session: Engaging Students Immediately

The first class session can set a positive tone for the semester, and deserves our special attention. While it is possible to recover from a mediocre first session and still organize a good semester, we are much better off showing students from the first meeting that the course will be informative and enjoyable. Once students have decided that the course is going to be a good one, they will be more willing team members. As well, once they're on our side they tend to be forgiving if we occasionally have a session that is a bit of a clunker.

There are certain administrative necessities of the first session, such as giving students information on policies and procedures and dealing with individuals on waiting-lists. While such paperwork is necessary, try not to let it take over the entire session. We recommend that you spend at least a few minutes on course content. This helps to spark students' interest in the material, motivate them to start reading, and inspire them to care about the concerns of the discipline. The session can be fast-paced, interesting, and involving. It can be orchestrated so students meet each other and experience some intriguing aspect of the course material. There are simple ways to accomplish this even if students are completely new to the discipline.

Consider setting up an expectation of interaction by having students meet a few people around them. We tell students: "You'll have copious opportunities this semester to speak with other students in this class. Let's start right now. For the next 30 seconds, please meet any two people here who you don't already know." Students quickly feel the positive results of interacting with others in the room, and any discomfort is short-lived. Keep such activities brief to allow the session to move forward at a good pace.

The first major item on the agenda is to introduce the syllabus and/or course outline containing the class schedule, operational details, departmental policies, and the like. This is an opportunity to immediately establish a participatory tone to the class. Rather than read a list of policies and procedures, rather than describe the schedule, term project, and exam details, why not have students ask you questions? This strategy illuminates an important general principle: For effective teaching, look for opportunities for questions and ideas to come from students rather than from you.

Set students up for this activity by telling them that their responsibility in the next few minutes is to discover what to expect in this course. Tell them you want their questions about anything to do with it—topics to be discussed, readings, exams, assignments, or their questions about you the instructor. Then ask students to form groups of three to four to examine the syllabus for a few minutes, generating a list of questions from their points of curiosity or concern. When time is up, remind them that all questions are acceptable. "Ask me anything, and don't worry if it might be answered somewhere on the handouts. Questions, please!" Many of their queries will be the usual suspects: "Is the final exam cumulative?" "Do we research the main project by ourselves or in groups?" "Are there any essays on the exams?" But you will be offering information in response to their needs rather than yours. And the experience will be a satisfying give-and-take rather than a monologue.

There will be some important policies that students will not ask about, such as plagiarism and missed assignments, and you should briefly review those with them. Emphasize the necessity that students read all handouts.

At some point, tell learners a little about yourself. Tell enough to show that you have the professional qualifications to be there. Show that you're enthusiastic about your field, and that you care about good teaching. Show that you have points of view, but that you welcome alternative opinions. And, without being inappropriately personal, show that you're human.

> *After outlining my professional qualifications I inform students that my academic career got off to a rocky start years ago when I was expelled from kindergarten for uncooperative behaviour. I also tell them that I failed out of first-year university. Both stories are true, and serve to humanize me as well as to reassure students whose academic paths have not been an unbroken series of successes. The stories also make them laugh, a welcome addition to the first day. —EB*

Learning Students' Names

Even if you are teaching very large classes, you will want to learn as many students' names as possible. We follow the practice of taking students' photographs on the first day of class. It requires a little time and trouble, but students are amazed at the results when you call them by name for the entire semester (and sometimes beyond). In our method, each class member fills out a large file card with personal background information. This is also a good opportunity for you to find out who your students are. Ask questions that will help you gear the class more specifically to them as individuals. You might ask for basic identification and a little relevant background: name, phone number, e-mail address, previous courses taken in the discipline, any work history related to the field, and outside interests. You might ask about travel experience or family history, especially if that would relate to the course. Then confess to students that you're about to take their pictures, and be prepared for groans and laughter.

Here are two possible ways to accomplish the picture-taking.

1. As students are writing their file cards, or afterward, group them into threes or fours and take their pictures. Take two photographs of each group, just be to be sure, but try to keep the procedure light, quick and even humorous. For a class of 40, the whole procedure requires about five minutes. At the end, collect the file cards. Next session, after you've had the film developed, bring in the cards plus the pictures, which you have cut into individual snapshots. Lay the materials on a table along with several tape dispensers, and ask students as they arrive for class to each pick his/her snapshot and card, tape the picture to the card, and hand it in. This method is extremely easy for you and provides you with a stack of photo-ID by the second session. You can then start memorizing names in preparation for the third session.[14]

2. An alternative method demands more time and attention, but has the benefit of allowing you to learn students' names by the beginning of the second class session. When at least some of the students have finished their file cards, ask them to come up to the front and have pictures taken in threes. Snap the pictures, then carefully collect the cards in the same order that you took the pictures. If you don't trust yourself to pick up the cards in order, ask students to write their names in bold pen on the backs of their cards (have several felt pens handy) and hold them up under their chins. One-hour film processing, a little tape, and you've got a complete set of file cards with snapshots.

Once we have the cards, we study them the night before the class and address students by name the next day. We sometimes make it dramatic by reciting the names of everyone in the class, and have occasionally been rewarded with a round of applause.

There are other ways of learning students' names. You can

have each individual meet another and introduce that person to the whole class. You can proceed through the entire room having students say their own names plus those of several other students. You can have students wear name-tags. Some instructors have students fill out file cards; then at the start of every class the instructor peruses the cards while scanning the class, trying to make connections. However, we find methods that employ photographs to be the most successful. If you are nervous about your lack of photographic skill or equipment, your university's audio-visual department may agree to take the pictures or loan you cameras or video-cams.

Introductory Activities

Icebreakers can be useful during the first session. There are countless varieties of these exercises, which are intended to introduce students to each other and increase the comfort level in the group. Some are personal, requiring students to meet others and play brief games or discuss extracurricular activities.

Although such activities can be useful, we suggest icebreakers that employ the course material. This may seem difficult on the first day of class, when students haven't even read chapter one. But students enter every discipline, no matter how exotic, with ideas, preconceptions, information, and misinformation. One exciting and motivating approach asks students to debate general-interest questions relating to the discipline.

This introductory exercise is similar to the Pairs Discussion technique for student participation, described in the next chapter. Bring to the first class three to six general-knowledge questions drawing on your discipline. We suggest that each question be word-processed in large type on an overhead transparency—one question per page.

Have students find partners. This is most easily accomplished by simply asking students to turn to someone next to them; however, tell them that threesomes are fine—you don't want individual students embarrassed to find themselves caught with no partner. Once students are in twos or threes, get their attention and tell them you are going to put a question on the overhead, which they are to discuss for only one minute. Tell them that during the minute, they should ensure that each member of the partnership has a chance to speak. Then turn on the machine, put up the question, read it aloud, and say "Go." Here are a few questions from Psychology and related disciplines that work well for this activity.[15]

- True or False? Couples who live together before marriage are more likely to later split up than couples who do not live together before marriage.
- True or False? On average, surveys show that people in their 20s and 30s generally report greater life satisfaction (say they're happier) than do people in their 60s and 70s.
- Heroin is more dangerous to health than is alcohol. Comment.
- Most people believe that we sleep "to rest," but psychologists say that explanation is inadequate. Why? Name any reasons that you can.
- You have a chance to play golf against Tiger Woods for a prize of $1 million. You really want to win. How many holes would you choose to play: 1, 9, 18, or 36? Why?

After allowing each group one minute to discuss a question, bring the class back together and debrief. You can take a show of hands or ask for comments. Keep it fast-paced, then move on to the next question. To make this exercise as successful as possible, show only one question at a time. That focuses students' attention and prevents their racing through questions without really thinking. If you want students to give full attention to each question, but also be able to take the questions away after class, distribute a handout following the exercise.

The best questions for this exercise are relevant to your discipline but require no expert knowledge; they do not have obvious answers and potentially generate a variety of responses. Such questions pique students' interest, expose them to different opinions, and allow them to anticipate issues that will emerge throughout the course. No matter what your field of study, you can devise questions that work for such an exercise. In linguistics, ask students to speculate on the origins of certain idiomatic expressions. In health sciences, ask students for some of the probable reasons for nursing shortages. In literature, ask students for a defensible distinction between prose and poetry. In community planning, ask students where municipal buildings are located around town, and possible reasons—social, economic, or political—for those locations. In introductory astronomy, ask students what they know about black holes. Or pose questions that are simply fun. In English literature, ask students to name as many Shakespeare plays as they can, or in chemistry as many elements from the periodic table as possible. The list is endless, the issues infinite. Remember the purposes of this exercise: to draw students into the issues of your discipline, and to motivate them to participate in their learning.

Plan an outline for the first session that allows you to accomplish your objectives. For a 50-minute class, here is one possible schedule:

00:00   Greetings from you. A few brief words about the course or discipline. Have students meet several others around them.

00:05   Direct students to the outline/course syllabus. Have them form groups of three to four, look over the syllabus and list questions about the course.

00:10   Take questions from students as a way of introducing the syllabus and course outline in detail.

00:20   Hand out large file cards. On overhead projector, show questions you would like them to answer about themselves.

00:25   Take photos.

00:35   Introductory exercise: Question #1. Students discuss in pairs, then debrief with whole class.

00:40   Question #2. Same as above.

00:45   Question #3. Same as above.

00:49   End class.

With classes longer than 50 minutes, you will be able to accomplish this at a slightly more leisurely pace. If you teach in large blocks of time (say, three to four hours at a stretch) you will want to follow the above-outlined session with a break and then begin teaching the course material. Whatever your overall schedule for the first day, you can involve students immediately in collaborative work that will engage them and leave them eager for the coming semester.

Chapter 13

Using Frequent
Participatory Techniques

Most students want to participate in classes, and we as instructors want them to as well. But meaningful and purposeful student involvement will not just happen automatically. The classroom is an unnaturally formal setting not conducive to active learning. The regimented seating, the uncomfortable chairs, and the dull bare walls conspire to lull students into passivity. We instructors are also constrained by our own traditional educational backgrounds and our fears that we will lose control over students and have trouble handling unfamiliar classroom situations. We particularly fear transition points, moving from lecture to activity and then back to lecture again, each of which requires that we regain our students' attention. It is tempting to avoid such situations, and simply start each class in lecture mode, then carry on without stopping. At the same time, though, we know that we are more effective teachers when we construct learning systems that engage students and access their latent creative energy.

Students are also more effective learners when they become actively involved with the academic material. That means engaging in discussion with other students and with the instructor, and taking part enthusiastically in intellectual exercises. We actually give students a little speech near the start of each semester, stating that they should have numerous goals at university. Those goals will include to gain knowledge, to become clearer thinkers, and to learn to express their ideas more articulately and confidently. We tell them they will more likely achieve those goals if they participate regularly in class discussions and activities.

You can best promote student participation by planning frequent, brief exercises to be interspersed throughout the session, rather than leaving such involvement until the end of class. Discussion is most lively and meaningful immediately after material has been presented. Furthermore, students are more energetic early in the session when they have not settled into passive roles and when they are not yet distracted by the clock and their next commitments.

Many different active-learning exercises have been developed for college classrooms, from games for testing factual knowledge, to simulations and debates for probing deeper ideas. You can collect ideas from colleagues or from books specifically describing such exercises. Here we present foundation strategies that can be used continuously throughout the semester, to establish an expectation among students of constant participation. These basic techniques can be used in classes of 20 or 500, and even in sterile classrooms with fixed seating.

Pairs Discussions

This simple but powerful technique ensures that every student in the room gets a chance to discuss some aspect of the course material in every class period. It is a preplanned and organized way of having students debate or verbalize on issues, using very little class time. It provides opportunities to have students learn from each other, and is especially suitable for courses that are largely lecture format.

The technique relies on class members working in pairs. That way, at any given time, half the students in the room are talking, all on-task and with no chaos. Some instructors prefer groups of three or four, for which the principles described here apply equally well.

The exercise creates a lot of noise and establishes an atmosphere of informality, which increases the comfort level in the classroom. Indispensable to the exercise are brief time-limits (1 minute, 2 minutes) which create excitement and encourage students to focus quickly on the heart of the question.

When planning a particular class session, choose one or more opportunities for student input and discussion. Plan for these to be scattered throughout the session rather than a few minutes before class ends. For each occasion, think of a question to ask students, and type it in large letters on a full-sized standard sheet of paper, on acetates, or word-processed into your laptop for overhead projection. Make the letters large (even 32-point or more), so students are not distracted by squinting to read it.

Perhaps that particular day you are discussing the European Union. After 20 minutes of an introductory lecture, ask each student to find a partner. Give them five seconds to introduce themselves. Tell them they'll have two minutes to discuss a question you will pose, during which time they should come up with as specific an answer as possible. Then project the question, read it aloud, and say "Go."

It can be a simple question asking students to summarize lecture information, it can be an application of the information, or it can be a more difficult analytical task. Almost any question, even a complex one, can be profitably discussed for short periods of time, although complex ones demand that you follow up later.

For best results, make the question as specific as possible. So rather than asking "What is your opinion of the European Union?" try "Why was the European Union formed? Without looking at your notes, name as many reasons as you can." You can ask a series of questions of increasing sophistication and difficulty, asking students to talk about each one in turn. So if you're teaching astronomy, after an introductory lecture on Jupiter you might first ask a basic question: "What are the chemical constituents of Jupiter's atmosphere?" Then a more difficult one: "How do we know that? In other words, what research methods were used to determine atmospheric components?" Then a yet more difficult one: "For those research methods, cite advantages and disadvantages, scientific or otherwise." All of these questions, especially the latter ones, demand extensive further discussion. But why not let students start the ball rolling?

You might want to ask questions that require students to develop opinions or use their judgment on some issue in the field. Phrase the question to encourage various points of view. For example: "Based on your readings and your reflection on American foreign-aid policy, do you think that policy has been more of a help or a hindrance to Asian economic development?"

Even questions whose answers appear self-evident are usefully discussed this way. For example, a geography instructor could start a class by asking pairs or groups of students to discuss "What exactly is the greenhouse effect?" While students would say "everybody knows" what the greenhouse effect is, few could verbally define it well. And students don't really know something (a fact, a phenomenon, a theory) unless and until they can articulate it in their own words.

This exercise can also be a motivating introduction to a lecture. Say you are about to talk about medical epidemiology. You might start the lecture by putting students in pairs and asking, from a clearly written question on the projector or overhead: "Multiple sclerosis is much more prevalent in temperate regions of the world than in tropical ones. Name as many factors as you can—geographical, social, or other—that epidemiologists might investigate to explain this phenomenon." You are asking students to anticipate your lecture, which will make them even more interested in, and personally committed to, the session as it unfolds.

As for the mechanics of forming pairs or groups, students find partners by turning to someone seated next to them, or by turning around to the row behind. Instructors should encourage students to make sure no individual is left out of a group. So, for example, when students are forming themselves into pairs, emphasize that threesomes are fine. You can facilitate this by physically moving around the classroom, addressing any individual students who are sitting alone and gently easing them into groups. An alternative method, which we occasionally use, is to ask students to get up and find someone in the room they have never met, and sit down to discuss the question. Students sometimes balk at being asked to move, but appreciate it afterward.

After students have talked in pairs, prepare to debrief with the whole class so students can share their best ideas. Get their attention, repeat the question to the class as a whole, and take suggested answers. Keep the discussion fast-paced and on track. If you're simply brainstorming, you will accept any and every answer, and leave assessment for later. Alternatively you may want to indicate which answers are closer to the mark than others. For more on facilitating discussions, see Chapter 23.

In summary, to make this exercise succeed:

- Come prepared with a question (one or more per class session). If you organize the question on the spot, you may lose momentum.
- Try to frame questions that have more than one answer or that encourage various points of view.
- Make sure each question is general enough to be interesting but specific enough to be answerable.
- Remind students that learning occurs best when they verbalize and reflect on information, and that these discussions will help them learn. It will inspire their enthusiasm for the exercise.
- Before showing the question, ensure that each student knows who his/her discussion partner is. Give them a few seconds to introduce themselves if they've never met before.
- Set a brief time limit (30 seconds, 1 minute, or 2 minutes) and inform students of it.
- Make sure your question is written on an overhead transparency or the board, in large letters that are easy to read even from the back of the room.
- Debrief by taking comments from the class as a whole.

*In my classes, I frequently ask questions for pairs
discussion. Occasionally it's a simple question to remind
them of their reading. Often it's a more complex query
to open up issues for discussion. For example, after a
brief lecture on clinical depression, I post the following
on the overhead: "Women are diagnosed as being
clinically depressed much more often than are men. Think
of as many possible explanations for this as you can."
Immediately, there's an enormous amount of noise in the
room, all of it on-task. —EB*

Brief Comments on Paper

This is a simple but useful technique for student involvement that can serve numerous purposes. It can form a basis for cooperative learning or class discussion, or allow you to assess the clarity of your own lecture. It can be employed at the beginning of class, partway through a lecture, or at the end.

This technique asks that students work alone for a moment collecting their thoughts and writing points on paper before discussing an issue with the class or with a partner. This has several advantages.

- It gives students a chance to sort out their own thoughts before discussion;
- It forces students to develop ideas and opinions themselves rather than always relying on others;
- It gives students writing practice;
- It provides you with a written sample of work to grade if you so choose;
- It can give learners a sense of their intellectual progress throughout the semester. You can ask students to write points of their own, then additional points from a pairs discussion, then any final points derived from a whole-class discussion. Each student will have a record of these, documenting the discussions throughout the course.

Suppose you try this after a half-hour of lecturing. It may be a macroeconomics session on federal money supply, a lecture on the philosophy of John Dewey, or a literature class on African-American fiction. At a natural break in the lecture, or after a particular unit of material, pass out paper and ask students to:

(a) Answer specific questions from the lecture without looking back at their notes.

(b) Summarize the main point of your lecture, in one or two sentences. If you dare, collect these and read them later to see how clear you were.

(c) Link the lecture with previous readings in some specific way.

(d) Ask you a question on any point that is unclear.

For these written comments, give students time limits. Once students have finished writing, you have several choices. Each individual can use it as a self-test, checking answers against their notes. Students can hand in the papers to give you information on what they understood from the lecture. You may even decide to grade the work, if you have warned students first and written it into your syllabus. After students have articulated their thoughts on paper, you can ask them to share their ideas in pairs or small groups; alternatively, you can resume whole-class discussion or lecture. However you follow it up, the writing activity has benefits for students and provides useful variety in the classroom.

It is amazing how much energy and how many ideas students demonstrate when you create encouraging learning environments. Punctuating your class with brief exercises will improve your lectures without taking much class time. It will allow students to be active rather than passive, and encourage them to interact with the material you present. The variety will increase the attention span of the class, and your students will be grateful for it. Once you have tried a few activities of this type, it is unlikely you will want to return to non-stop lecturing.

Chapter 14

Case Studies and Problem-Based Learning

While frequent and brief exercises can supply most of the student involvement in your class, from time to time you may want to devote a larger chunk of time to lengthier and deeper participatory methods.

One such method uses case studies—complex, real-life narratives that students read and discuss, which require that they think deeply about issues important in the course.[16] The value of case studies has become widely recognized since their development at the Harvard Business School, and they are now used in academic and professional programs at numerous institutions. In recent years some universities have moved full-tilt into this teaching approach and turned one or more programs almost entirely over to what is now frequently called problem-based learning (PBL). In problem-based learning, professors do little or no lecturing but facilitate a process in which students work in groups during class applying textbook theory, outside information, and their own analysis to realistic problems.

Basically an extension of the case-study method, PBL has inspired considerable enthusiasm in higher education. While teaching with such narratives sounds and is exciting, it is considerably different from traditional teaching and raises its own challenges. Among potential problems: some students feel they learn less in PBL courses than in lecture ones; evaluation is more complex in PBL than in traditional lecture courses; and assigning students equitably to long-term groups is difficult to do.[17] As well, if an administrative decision has been made to change an entire program to PBL (or to make any other such extreme change), professors are forced on short notice to revamp their teaching, in the process discarding not only ineffective methods, but effective ones too.

If you develop interest in trying case studies or problem-based learning, we suggest that you proceed cautiously and gradually, and not abandon your previous teaching strategies. In our opinion, professors can reap the benefits of problem-based learning without inviting the difficulties, by interspersing ordinary lecture or seminar courses with occasional case-study activities. This allows us to fulfil our roles as providers and synthesizers of information, while allowing students scope to generate and apply ideas.

A case study, then, is a narrative that might describe:

- an ethical dilemma in which an archaeologist must decide how to handle controversial cultural items;
- an engineering task of designing a highway in a major city in which scientific decisions will be affected by political realities;
- a situation in which retailers must determine how to advertise their product most effectively in an unusually difficult market;
- the quandary of a youth worker dealing with kids who have fallen into drugs and prostitution;
- a simple description of an everyday problem in any realm—social, health, or professional—a discussion of which would benefit students.

The best case studies are relevant to the course material, are plausible, involve realistic characters (neither all-good nor all-bad), are engaging, describe situations requiring difficult decisions, have no obvious, easy solutions, and lend themselves to discussion and to different points of view.

You may be able to access case studies from books, through colleagues, or through your wider discipline group. You can also consider writing your own. Case studies do not have to be beautifully written. They do not have to be perfect. They simply need to contain elements that will allow students to see how the issues of the discipline play out in real life.

Neither do cases need to be lengthy to be useful. You can write short narratives only a few paragraphs long containing sufficient information for a discussion. Besides taking less time to write, short narratives have one important advantage over long ones: you can distribute them at the beginning of class and have students read them quickly.

One short narrative that Eleanor wrote for a psychology course begins: "Emma is a 40-year-old woman who lives under the bridge, surrounded by garbage and abandoned cars. Emma has schizophrenia." A fictional account of a mentally ill woman, de-institutionalized and homeless, this one-page story describes her personal history. The story shows how compassionate and caring have been the relevant individuals in her life—her family, mental-health professionals, and psychiatric hospital staff. Yet here she is, living alone and ragged, under the bridge. The situation calls for examination of society's, and individuals', responsibilities to Emma and to other troubled people. Using the case study as a vehicle, students engage in such examination using details of the story, information from previous readings and lectures, and their own compassion and analysis. Through discussion they grasp some of the complexities of social issues.

If you decide to use a lengthy case, you will want to ensure that students read it before class. Should you find less-than-adequate compliance you may want to start giving students a short quiz on the case at the beginning of the class. Though this may sound distastefully coercive, remember that small-group discussions are unsatisfying when only two students of a group of four actually did the assigned reading.

Once students have read the case, the ensuing discussion should be structured for maximum effectiveness. Discussion is usually best accomplished first in small groups, then with the class as a whole. You might consider having small-group work proceed as follows: Each group chooses a chairperson whose task it is to keep the discussion on track and keep an eye on the clock. If you prefer, this can be seen as two separate tasks for two different individuals. Each group also chooses a recorder whose task it is to write down ideas—either every idea that is generated, or ones that the group decides are substantive. We suggest that you distribute at the outset a short list of questions to form the basis of the small-group discussions.

The questions can be as challenging and sophisticated as you like, if you have considerable class time and your group is prepared to use its time well in this non-traditional learning. Most simply, however, you might use your own variant of the following:

- What are the basic facts of the case? Tell the story in your own words, briefly but including all important details.
- What are the problems for the individuals here? What values or needs are in conflict?
- What are possible options for the main participants? What are possible solutions to the problem(s)? What knowledge or expertise can you bring to the case from the course material?
- What are the consequences (positive and negative) of each option? Which options do you think are best? Why?

What you are asking students to do, then, is the following:

- Summarize the case. This is necessary so that discussion will not be sidetracked by arguments over questions of fact.
- Define the problem(s). Just as any group of people, whether social workers or corporate managers, cannot solve a problem until they agree on what it is, so students

must concur on the basic dilemma(s) before venturing further.

- Identify possible solutions, especially using information or ideas from the course. Coach students to accept any and all ideas from their group members, in the manner of brainstorming.
- Assess those suggested solutions. List pros and cons or positive and negative consequences of each, then decide which solutions are likely to be best.

During the small-group work, you can circulate to help keep discussions productive and on track. Some instructors like to pull up a chair and briefly join groups while others, concerned that students may be intimidated by their presence, prefer to scan from the front of the classroom. Whatever physical position you choose, make sure it allows you to monitor the room for the crucial task of troubleshooting. If any groups are sitting in silence or otherwise not functioning, we suggest you join them and ask questions, make comments, or occasionally even change the composition of a group to get it moving again.

The small-group discussions can take anywhere from a few minutes to an hour or more, depending on the complexity of the case. After that, get everyone's attention and begin the class debriefing. The whole-class discussion can move, one by one, through the same four questions that participants discussed in their groups. For each one, listen to answers and take note (on the overhead or the board) of those most likely to lead to solutions. Watch the time and keep the discussion moving. Bear in mind your objectives, which include to have students:

- realize that most problems do not lend themselves to simple solutions;
- practise articulating ideas, cooperating, and sharing information;
- practise listening to others' opinions and gaining respect for diverse views;

- learn to take a variety of points of view into account in problem-solving;
- criticize constructively by analyzing possible solutions to a problem;
- develop their own educated opinions in your discipline.

Case studies are opportunities for students to discuss course material in relation to realistic problems. Students find them fascinating and challenging, and appreciate the opportunity to discuss genuine applications of your academic field to real life.

Chapter 15

Student Presentations: Making Them Work

Many instructors ask students to give class presentations, which are potentially excellent learning experiences. But presentations must be thought out clearly in advance or they can present a perilous combination of disadvantages. If poorly planned and executed, student presentations are demoralizing for presenters, excruciating for other class members, and wasteful of class time. On the other hand, if the presentation structure is well-planned (by instructors) the experiences can be satisfying for presenters, and enriching for listeners. Depending on how you organize the presentations, they don't even have to use up much class time.

Why include student presentations in a class? For any student, giving a presentation can be a useful experience in expressing academic concepts as well as an opportunity to gain valuable practice in public speaking. It ensures that the student has more than a superficial understanding of an issue. Presentations by learners also provide variety in class and make a course more student-centred.

Despite all of these reasons to include student presentations in our classes, caution is required. There are two types of problems associated with presentations, one relating to form, the other to quality of content. First, students' shyness, nervousness, lack of experience, and lack of public-speaking skills can sometimes combine to make the experience torturous for both presenters and listeners. Second, if the presentation contains information that you have not covered in your lecture, then for the sake of other learners it must be presented accurately and comprehensibly. Presentations work best when the material is not otherwise covered in readings or lecture. Consequently, we suggest that you do not test the class on material presented by students unless you first check their research for accuracy.

If you want learners to present information to classmates, you have several basic choices of structure.

1. Individual students present to the entire class.

    The most common method of presentation in university seminars and college classes, this structure nevertheless has drawbacks—it is stressful for presenters and takes up a large amount of class time. After all, if a student gives a 10-minute presentation to 50 students, the presentation has taken 500 minutes of student time.

    To use this method most effectively, remember two crucial points. First, emphasize the importance of brevity. Second, since most undergraduates are unskilled at presenting information publicly, speak in class about the elements of effective public speaking. Your points might include those in the list at the end of this chapter. Do this before student presentations begin; it will be embarrassing to students and therefore diplomatically impossible after several poor presentations have been done. For more on mentoring student presenters, see Chapter 16.

2. Small groups of students present to the entire class.

    In this method, groups of students prepare for the presentation by studying a particular topic together. On the appointed day, they all go to the front of the class; in their allotted few minutes, each group member speaks. The advantages to this method are that it gives students experience in cooperative group work, it takes less class time overall, and members of the presentation groups are less nervous because they are not presenting alone. Disadvantages include that group presentations require meetings outside class, which busy students often have trouble accomplishing. Another disadvantage is that one or more members often feel they have done more than their share of the work, a dilemma common to group projects.

To optimize this method, remind students of the value of learning to work together. Keep groups small and encourage students to break the project into segments, each of which can be researched to some extent on its own. Some instructors also ask group members (anonymously on paper) to assess the contribution of each member to the project in percentage terms. You may then use this information in evaluation. However, students sometimes feel uncomfortable with this, and if their assessments are wildly divergent it can complicate your evaluation decisions.

3. Individuals present to small numbers of classmates.

This combines the advantages of the first two methods, and also provides a forum in which students can work cooperatively. But it does require careful logistical planning on your part.[18]

In this arrangement, you designate a particular class-date as Presentation Day, on which every class member will present to a small group of other students. In each particular group, every student will present on a different but related topic.

The essence of this method is that students learn from each other. For example, if you want learners to become conversant with six journal articles, arrange to have six students per group with each individual presenting on a different article. Alternatively, if you are discussing a topic that lends itself to various theoretical approaches, have each student in a group present on a different approach. Or perhaps a topic divides neatly into several sub-topics; if so, have each student in a group present on one of those sub-topics. For instance, in a health-sciences class you might arrange for each member of a group to present on a separate disorder.

As you plan for this activity, divide the class into groups of about five students each, with x number of groups depending on the size of your class. A few weeks before the presentations, give the class a number of topics from which each student chooses one. Each learner does the necessary research independently, then prepares a presentation of 5 to 15 minutes (depending on the length of your class session) plus one to two questions for group discussion. Because no two individuals in a given group should present on the same topic, you will need at least five different presentation topics (the number of people in each group) and you will need to ensure that no more than x (the number of groups) students sign up for each topic. After individuals have chosen topics, you then assign students to groups, ensuring no overlap of topics within a given group.

On Presentation Day, make sure that tables and chairs are arranged into groups, and have each student find his/her group from lists you have posted. Instruct groups to decide in what order their members will present, and let them get started. The following added instructions also inspire students to rigour and involvement:

(a)   Each group should appoint a timekeeper to ensure that individual presenters do not take more than their allotted time for presentation plus discussion.

(b)   When a student is presenting, others in the group have the important task of listening and supporting the speaker. Students should not be putting the finishing touches on their own work while another group member is presenting. It is every individual's responsibility to help other presenters by being attentive, asking questions, and taking an active part in the discussions.

Because there are a number of groups scattered around the room, numerous people are speaking at any one time—one in each group. The structure results in a lot of noise and energy, and is an entertaining means of giving students a presentation experience. Anxiety levels are lower because students are presenting to only a few others. Student presenters cannot be heard by anyone outside their own group. The low-stress format also results in more participation from other students, who are more likely to make comments and ask questions in front of three to five others than in front of 30 or 60. And it takes relatively little class time.

The main disadvantage of this method is that evaluating the students is difficult. Because there are numerous presentations occurring simultaneously, you will find it challenging to assess them. You can address this by (a) evaluating each presentation yourself on the basis of a quick scan of the proceedings, or (b) evaluating students largely on the basis of a written summary that they submit to you, then simply giving each student a few points for completing the presentation. Another option is to have students evaluate each others' presentations, but we do not recommend this. In our experience, students lack the background and knowledge to evaluate their peers effectively, and find it awkward to be asked to do so.

Whatever method you choose, give students specific guidelines for doing high-quality presentations. These might include:

- Know your topic, but avoid excessive detail. Be clear on the main points you wish to make.
- Stick to your time limit. Have a plan for your talk, for example, five minutes for Topic A, then five minutes for Topic B, then a discussion question to the audience, then a summary of your main ideas.
- Try not to read your presentation to the audience. Have your main points written in note form on cards to which you can refer. Then speak in a conversational style, referring to these points.

- Use visual aids if that is appropriate, and use them well. Bring graphs, pictures, books, or any props that are relevant and that will bring the information alive for the group. Project or display them in a way that allows everyone to see.
- Incorporate some way to involve your audience. Prepare one or two questions to ask other students. Encourage comments and discussion during or after your presentation.
- Relax and have fun. Your audience will enjoy it more and will learn more, too.

Chapter 16

Organizing Effective Seminar Classes

S eminar classes are opportunities for intensive student involvement and for practice in academic discourse and debate. Whether graduate or undergraduate they are most often small classes of 20 or fewer individuals, affording students more chances to articulate their ideas and learn through inquiry. When they work, seminar classes are an inspiring embodiment of the educational ideal. However, seminars do not always work so well in practice. Sometimes they consist of aimless discussion in which participants later feel little was achieved. Other times they are dominated by one or two opinionated individuals. Often they consist largely of presentations by students who have not been coached in delivering material effectively.

There are a number of reasons that some courses or classes are held as a seminar or discussion group. For example, enrolment may be small because the course is in a specialized program; in this case you expect a small number of students and can plan for it. In other cases enrolment is unexpectedly low; if you plan for 30 students but only get 10, you may decide to run it largely as a discussion group.

Seminars may form a portion of a larger course that also has a lecture component; the seminars complement the lectures and provide a forum for student discussion. In our experience, a major mistake in leading such seminars is that facilitators (whether teaching assistants or faculty members) often see the sessions as question-and-answer periods requiring little preparation. We have known of seminars that proceeded as follows:

> Leader: Hi, everybody. This week the professor talked in the lecture about the influence of ethnic and class conflict on Latin American politics. Does anyone have any questions on the lecture or the readings?
>
> Students: (Uncomfortable silence)
>
> Leader: Does anybody have any questions? Someone must have a question.

Occasionally a student musters a comment to break the log jam, and sometimes the leader does so. But such seminars often end early, and can be highly unsatisfying.

Seminars should not exist solely for student questions, unless you are prepared to take the step of specifically requiring each student to bring one or more well-thought-out questions to the seminar each week, and structure the class around those queries. This approach has its benefits, but it takes the seminar out of your hands. While you may feel that issues A and B are the most important of the week, student questions may focus on issues C and D. A good seminar should leave plenty of time for student questions, but it should be like any class—well-prepared and clearly planned to cover the important topics, while allowing students to explore issues, express opinions, and work out ideas in groups of peers.

Another type of seminar is that which is part of a professional program, perhaps as an adjunct to practicum work. One common mistake here is using the session primarily for housekeeping, as a business meeting rather than an academic seminar, for example: "How's everybody's practicum going? Do you know how to fill out these forms to submit to the graduate studies department?" We believe such sessions should, instead, be used primarily to explore deeper ideas. These might involve applying theory on the job, working with a particular clientele, or discussing the major skill components of the work being learned.

Alternatively, you may teach a graduate seminar that is deliberately kept small for the sake of in-depth discussions on research methods or content in the field. Major mistakes in leading such seminars are that leaders do not prepare sufficiently, give too few instructions, and exercise too little leadership in discussion. Seminar leaders in graduate classes sometimes arrive with no plan other than to "get discussion going" on a particular reading. But that rarely produces a satisfying session. If any one of us was chairing a business meeting, we would never come without an agenda listing items that were important to cover. Similarly we as instructors should come to a seminar with well-thought-out plans.

No matter what kind of seminar you are teaching, a few basic points will help make it a good educational experience.

1. As in any course, a seminar course should be built on an overall vision including clear objectives. Do you want students to understand theories, gain skills, or develop new attitudes? As part of your planning, write objectives for yourself.

2. Readings, assignments, and discussions should be chosen carefully. Give students clear reasons to read particular works, and guidance in the form of questions to answer or issues to think about while reading.

3. Discussions must be structured and facilitated so that important ideas emerge and all class members are participating.

4. If student presentations are part of the course, seminar participants should be guided in how to present material effectively.

Say you are teaching a course on wildlife ecology. One week early in the semester, you plan to ask students to read a research article on the destruction of wildlife habitat. At the end of the previous week's seminar, refer to the article and put it into context. You can direct learners to consider particular issues while reading: (a) specific causes for the disappearance of habitat; (b) research methods used by the authors; (c) a critique of those methods; and (d) possible solutions to the problem of habitat loss.

In the next session, your discussion of the article will focus on these four issues. Naturally you will make room for spontaneous and unforeseen points. But by and large you can structure the discussion around the subjects you have asked them to ponder. So your 1.5-hour seminar might be structured as follows:

00:00	Quick contextual overview from you.
00:05	Group discussion of specific causes for the disappearance of habitat.
00:20	Discussion of research methods used by the authors.
00:35	Critique of research methods.
00:50	Discussion of possible solutions to habitat problem.
01:05	Comments and questions from students.
01:20	Summary of main points.
	Introduction to article for next session.
01:30	End of session.

For each section of the above schedule, have a brief plan. Based on your objectives, what do you want students to take home from the discussion? What controversies do you want them to understand? What issues do you hope they will raise? Based on that, what question(s) will you ask to get the discussion started, and how will you follow-up to guide it? Try not to schedule the time too tightly. Discussion of a particular point almost always takes longer than you anticipated.

This is not to say you won't be flexible. Flexibility is important. We sometimes come to a class with a discussion idea we believe is central to the material, only to find that students are fascinated by—and want to explore—a different idea altogether. When that occurs, we should allow time for it. However, even after the most productive digressions, bring the class back to your plan.

If you do not prepare and structure the discussion, it will be a free-for-all in which crucial ground may or may not be covered. If you simply ask for comments and questions, the student who speaks first often sets the agenda for the first half-hour or more, sometimes focused on a point that is not important in the larger scheme of things. Of course students are intelligent and knowledgable. But you know more than they do about the field, and need to show leadership in the discussion. Most students want instructors to show leadership, too.

One other problem with unstructured seminars is that only a few students may participate. We have all been in a seminar in which one or more students dominate the discussion because of their life-experience or background in the field or because they are particularly assertive. It is difficult for other students to do anything about incessant talkers—only the instructor has the authority (and the responsibility) to rein them in. The flip-side is a problem as well—students who do not speak at all or who need special encouragement to do so. For ideas on obtaining balanced participation in class discussions, see Chapter 23.

When a discussion gets rolling, consider keeping a speakers' list. Especially when numerous students wish to express opinions, it sometimes happens that nobody is listening to the points being made because everyone is waiting for the speaker to conclude so they can pounce. It is your task to set up a situation that allows students to listen to each other. Keeping a speakers' list is straightforward. Have a pad of paper ready. When a student wishes to contribute, s/he catches your attention with a hand in the air and you add his/her name to the list. You facilitate by asking students to speak in the order in which their names appear on the list. It lowers students' anxiety because they know they will indeed get their opportunity. An alternative method is to move in a circle around the room and ask that everyone speak in their turn. This approach has limitations, however. Individuals may feel embarrassed and on the spot when their turn arrives, or they may not have much to say at that time but have a strong point to make five minutes later. As well, this structure may inhibit natural discussion because students do not feel free to respond immediately to others' comments; once their turn arrives their response may seem irrelevant.

You as the instructor should guide the discussion and frequently insert your own questions and comments. However, we caution against arguing and debating with students. The seminar exists so students can test their ideas against each other and gain facility in verbalizing thoughts and opinions. Instructors have advantages of superior knowledge, experience, and power. Students may not argue with an instructor for fear of the consequences at evaluation time. Even graduate students are aware of the power of the professor—perhaps even more so than undergraduates because grad-school relationships are more intense and the students have more to lose. It also wastes valuable seminar time when the professor carries on a debate with one student. Instead of entering the debate fully, use probing questions to help a student clarify or reassess his ideas.

Presentations

Many instructors design their seminars so that each student takes a turn giving a presentation and facilitating a discussion on a particular topic. There are several important organizational steps we can take to ensure that this is an effective learning experience for students.

First, think carefully about how you will assign specific topics to each student. This is often accomplished on the first day of the seminar, which can be a mistake. Sometimes the seminar leader runs through the topics verbally, asking students to call out: "Okay, who would like to present two weeks from today on Noam Chomsky?" . . . "Jason, you'd like to do that? Great. Next, who would like to present three weeks from today on . . . ?" In another version of this, students rush to the front and attempt to sign up for their preferred topic, or grab the article they would like to review. These approaches have one advantage: they get topics assigned quickly. However, they can be frustrating as well as stressful, and do not guarantee that students will receive topics that are optimal for them. Few students are certain on the first day of class which topics will coincide most closely with their interests. As well, the most assertive students usually snap up the most popular topics. You might consider allowing students to think about possible ideas for a few days, then submit their first, second, and third choices, from which you allocate. You can even ask them to give one-sentence reasons for their choices, to help in your decisions. For example, Eleanor has had students research a psychoactive drug for presentation in a pharmacology session. Some students chose to research a particular drug because they had a personal connection with it—a family member who takes an antidepressant, or a friend who often smokes marijuana. Others chose to research a particular drug only because they had heard of it. In a case like this, knowing the reasons for student choices can help the instructor assign topics more meaningfully. That said, there are times when you will want to leave topic choices entirely to students, as when there are so many alternatives that all participants will end up with topics that appeal to them.

Second, help students improve the quality of their presentations. A wonderful idea in theory, presentations are sometimes painful in practice both to the person at the front of the room and to those held captive. The vast majority of students need guidance on how to present academic material well. Some instructors start the semester by modelling a good presentation. That's a valuable idea, but we can do even more. After you have delivered a presentation, walk students through it. Explain how you organized your talk. Show them the skeleton notes to which you referred during the session. Remind them of what questions you asked to involve the group, and describe what makes some questions more effective than others. Discuss the importance of brevity, and explain why you included certain types of detail while omitting others. If you're brave, point out one or two teaching errors that you made (there will always be a few) and tell students what you should have done or said. Share with them that teaching is impossible to do perfectly, but possible for anyone to do well with some forethought.

We also remind students of the importance of their learning to speak and present information in public, and give them specific pointers such as those listed at the end of Chapter 15.

One last caution. If your goal for a seminar is to have students discuss possible solutions to a problem, do not introduce the session by giving a list of your own suggested solutions. That will deprive them of important learning opportunities. In a seminar, there is nothing wrong with the instructor offering a few well-organized comments to put ideas into context and to set the stage. Just be sure you do not undermine discussion by making points that would be better generated by students.

Chapter 17

Using Last Semester's Notes, but Bringing Them Alive First

Once you have taught a course, it really will be easier next time. That does not mean you will teach the course precisely the same way next semester. You may make considerable revisions. But your notes from last semester should provide a guide. No matter how fatigued you are after a class, therefore, try to resist the temptation to throw your lecture notes into a drawer, ostensibly to be filed when you have time. We urge that you establish a workable filing system, either physical or digital. After each class, tuck away your lecture notes and supporting materials—class handouts, overheads, exams plus answer keys—someplace you will actually be able to find them again. The filing will take much more time and be less accurate if you leave it until the end of term. Organizing paper may not be the most pleasant part of the job, but it is imperative. We say this from the bitter experience of having started from scratch in our planning more than once. We also suggest that you take five minutes after each class to make notes on your lecture plan regarding what worked well and what needs to be revised for next time. You may not remember a year later when teaching the course again. You may not even remember next week when planning a follow-up session on the topic.

There are numerous possible organizing systems. Filing chronologically works for some people, especially if they cover the material in roughly the same order each semester. Other instructors prefer a topic-based system, so the lecture on basic genetics gets one file folder while the lecture on genetic engineering gets another. You can devise any system, more or less sophisticated, as long as it works for you. Whether you have stored the materials on your hard drive or in your filing cabinet, your system should allow you to easily retrieve your notes on a given topic and see how you treated it last time around.

However, while you will want to consult your old notes when next teaching the course, it is important that you not simply pull them out of file folders and run to class. Last semester's class may have been a good one, but it won't be this year unless you make it come alive for you today.

We suggest rewriting your lecture plan anew each semester, for several reasons. First, the act of word-processing or hand-writing the plan will force you to think it through, and ensure that it is lively and relevant. Second, it is unlikely you will want to use exactly the same plan. You may want to re-order topics, or take more time to outline some current controversy in the field. You may have taught an earlier topic slightly differently this year, requiring that you now fill in extra background material for the new lecture. Your current students may have different experiences or interests than did last year's group. For one reason or another, you will want to revise at least a little. If you revise last year's plan without rewriting it, you will end up crossing out sections, drawing arrows between others, adding annotations, and generally creating a confusing plan. And that will compromise your goal of being and feeling organized. Third, as the historians among you will appreciate, it's nice to have a record of your plans from previous semesters so you can see how you have progressed.

When planning a lecture from last year's notes, ask yourself:

- Are this year's students different from last year's in having fewer (or more) prerequisites, or in some other way? Did you assign them new outside readings that might affect their understanding of this lecture?

- Are you presenting the course topics in the same order this year? If not, do this year's students need any additional background to the lecture?
- Have your own priorities about the field changed due to your recent research or reading?
- Are you teaching in a different classroom this year or have logistics or physical circumstances changed in a way that could have an impact on the class?

Ask yourself whether you should add new ideas and sub-topics, and remove any from last year that in retrospect now seem expendable. Re-order if necessary for maximum clarity and impact. Ask yourself what is occurring in your discipline this year (or, if you're in information technology or neuroscience, this week!) that might be included to make the class as current as possible. All of this may take as little as 15 minutes, though it could take considerably longer. But it will make the difference between an average class and one that is animated, fluent, and natural.

If you're a beginning instructor, you may find it hard to imagine just grabbing last year's notes and dashing to class. But the temptation sets in after a few semesters. And for all of us who have done it, we find ourselves at some moment during the class standing there with 50 sets of eyes upon us as we frown at our notes, wondering: "Where did these come from? What was I thinking?" Or at some point in the lecture chiding ourselves for not devising a more powerful example than that tired one that students did not understand last year, and probably won't this year either.

The same applies to quizzes and examinations. We all pull out last year's test as a foundation for this year's midterm. By all means make use of your previous hard work. But we need to look carefully over old exams before using them without revision. You may not have covered the identical material this year or in quite the same way. Many of us have found ourselves, in the middle of an exam, having to interrupt students and announce sheepishly, "Please ignore Question 14. We didn't cover that topic"—then scrambling to find a way for students to earn an extra point to make up for the cancelled question. It's not the end of the world, but it feels disorganized and unprofessional.

Fortunately, such scenes are avoidable. Make your lecture notes, exams, and other materials come alive for you each year, to create satisfying teaching and learning experiences.

Chapter 18

Guest Speakers and Field Trips

Every class appreciates a good guest speaker. Guest speakers increase diversity in the classroom and give students a point of view different from yours. They give students a window to another aspect of the field and sometimes to the outside world. The best guest speakers do these things informatively and entertainingly. And, since your institution probably has no budget for honoraria, the best ones also speak for free. The lack of budget for such professional necessities is, of course, no joking matter. But whether you can compensate speakers or not, you want to find effective ones.

Guest speakers should possess characteristics that will probably include: professional expertise, personal experience which allows them to say what a situation is really like, or a status which confers special credibility. If you want your students to feel the pathos of palliative care nursing, bring in the supervisor of the local hospice. If you want students to understand the complexities of defending a person accused of a serious crime, bring in a lawyer who has done that. If you want students to comprehend the difficulties of translating literature, bring in a person who has translated Spanish poetry into English. If you want students to become aware of the subtleties of running an election campaign, bring in a local party organizer. We suggest you not be shy about inviting guest speakers to your classroom. Even the busiest and most prominent individuals often enjoy sharing their experiences.

But while expertise, experience, or credibility may be necessary conditions, they are not sufficient for your bringing in the speaker. Try to determine whether the individual will be effective in the classroom. Is the person likely to be engaging? If s/he has done a lot of public presentations to non-specialist groups, it's probable. (This is not to say that novice public speakers are necessarily ineffective.) Is she naturally gregarious or otherwise personable? Is he likely to be open to the needs of the group? Is the person sensitive and diplomatic, not likely to offend students with inappropriate comments or jokes?

Your planning should include a thorough briefing with the guest speaker.

1. Let her know what topic you want her to discuss, what your objectives are, and what you hope students will get out of the experience. Make sure it is the topic that she wants, and is prepared, to discuss. Many's the guest appearance that has foundered on this lack of concordance.

2. Be specific about time. Do you want her to speak for 10 minutes or an hour? Can a question-and-answer session go longer? Plan for the class to end 5 minutes early so students can come up and chat with the speaker, thank her personally, and ask further questions. It will be more satisfying for the speaker if students are not forced to hurry away to other classes.

3. Let her know what kind of class it is—how much background students have in the topic and whether they tend to be quiet or involved.

4. Determine whether he likes to take questions throughout the presentation or wait until afterward.

5. Gather enough biographical detail for a short introduction. Check out your introduction to ensure that you won't undermine the presentation or embarrass him, particularly if the individual is not accustomed to public speaking,

6. Give him accurate and detailed directions on how to get to campus, where to park, where you will meet him and when. Suggest he give himself lots of time to get there. It's anxiety-provoking for everyone when a guest speaker is late.

As part of your planning, have a lecture or alternative class prepared. In our experience it is rare that a guest speaker fails to show up, but it happens.

Prime students for the speaker at least one session beforehand. Be enthusiastic, emphasize the importance that they attend the session, and remind them to be on time. Tell students whether detailed information from the presentation will be examinable, so they will know whether to take notes. We prefer to instruct students not to take notes but to concentrate on listening; later we post our own extensive notes for students to copy. If necessary, outline any rules of respect toward the speaker if you have concerns that the individual's controversial beliefs, unusual physical appearance, or any other factor might elicit inappropriate reactions from students.

On the day of the presentation, bring a bottle of water for the speaker and make sure the environment is clean and comfortable. You might give the speaker a clear table on which to spread his notes, and a stool in case he prefers not to stand throughout. Write the person's name on the board, indicating how she likes to be addressed, which will encourage students to ask questions. Introduce the speaker briefly. Your introduction should be formal enough to be respectful to the guest, but personable and enthusiastic. It should include a few words on the speaker's expertise or experience, including any praiseworthy information that the person would never mention himself. Include a short anecdote if it adds to students' understanding of the individual. However, it is unnecessary and unwise to be biographically comprehensive. Thank the speaker, who has taken her valuable time to be there. Tell students whether to ask questions during the presentation or afterward, based on the stated wishes of your speaker. At the close of your introduction, give students a chance to clap for the speaker with a simple, "Let's welcome Dr. Kleinfelt," initiating the clapping yourself as you leave centre stage.

We recommend you sit far to the back or to the side, so students are not looking to you during the presentation. Take detailed notes, which you can later make available to students and from which you can debrief during the next class to ensure that students understood the main points. Hopefully the speaker will be skilled and on track, but if not, you'll have a tricky situation: Should you interrupt a speaker who has gone far off on a tangent or who is neglecting the agreed-upon topic? In our view, it is acceptable for you to interrupt the speaker gently and ask a few pointed questions to bring the presentation back on track. It is also completely acceptable for you to give time warnings to make sure the speaker will wrap up as agreed and leave time for questions. While you want to be respectful to your guest, your main responsibility is to your students. Furthermore, giving time warnings saves the speaker the discomfort of having students slip out of the room for their next classes before he has concluded.

After question-and-answer, walk to the front of the room and thank the speaker properly. Try not to sound prepackaged. Demonstrate that you were listening by referring specifically to one or two of the main points. Close the session by giving students a structured opportunity to create a round of applause that will provide a natural ending to the class. Do not then try to regain students' attention for announcements. If you have announcements, make them earlier, before the speaker is introduced, or (if an announcement is brief) just prior to the formal thank-you at the end.

Ideally, the speaker will be an informative addition to the course. If the speaker was ineffective, not only have you lost a class session but you will have to decide whether to re-teach the material. We recommend that you do so, quickly in the next session, in the guise of a review. On the rare occasion when a speaker has been really poor, we have let students know we were disappointed in the quality of the presentation, to empathize with them and to preserve our own credibility.

Field Trips

Another way to provide variety and unusual experience is through field trips. We have organized many field trips, and can attest to the fact that, time-consuming as they are for instructors to organize and attend, they can be extremely valuable and memorable. A few tips:

- Start early in the semester to think about possible trips and begin organizing.
- Think out the logistics. Should the trip take place during or outside of class time? If outside of class time, should the activity be compulsory?
- If you will be using an external guide (such as a professional from the organization in question), speak to the person beforehand. Apprise the individual of the extent of the students' background and what you hope to achieve from the session. If you have your doubts that s/he is likely to be an effective guide, try to lead part of the tour yourself.
- Verbally list any useful rules of conduct for students, such as "Please don't touch the expensive equipment," or "Please don't give cigarettes to the inmates."

As with any educational activity, structure the field trip for maximum learning. We sometimes give students small individual handouts. These include maps they can follow and questions for them to answer as they gather information on the tour. Though this technique was originally developed for younger students, we have found it can be readily adapted to the university level, as a way to ensure that an activity is purposeful rather than unfocused. To make up such handouts, it helps to have visited the facility yourself in advance. It can be a brief visit, but take a few notes.

Field trips take large amounts of students' (and instructors') time. Make sure a particular trip meets one or more of the course objectives you established at the start of the semester.

Often you would like to take students to a location, event, or institution that cannot accept a group the size of your class. You have several choices, including to organize more than one trip there, or to divide the class into groups. However, it may be impossible for you or your TAs to go on multiple outings. And field trips proceed more smoothly if the instructor or a TA is present. Other options are to find a different field trip or make the activity optional and available only to a certain number of students who sign up first or who meet some specific criteria.

Finally, field trips need not be to faraway locations to be interesting. There may be opportunities right on your campus— an archaeology lab, the childcare centre, or the botanical greenhouses.

Chapter 19

Ending Classes on an Upbeat Note

It is satisfying to end a class a minute or two early, having discussed the most important information and brought the class to an organized close, with time to say: "That's all for today. Have a great evening. See you next time." There's a buzz in the classroom, and everybody's looking forward to the next session. —HR

If your class is supposed to end at 10:20 a.m., it should end at 10:19. Roughly speaking. While you do not want to consistently end the class much earlier than scheduled (giving the impression that you do not value the course, or have little to say), students will resent your chronically insisting that they stay late to hear a few last hurried points. In our experience, if your class is scheduled to end at 2:50 p.m., there is no use trying to convey information at 2:51, when students have stopped listening. We have all committed this teaching error, on the excuse that "there's so much material to cover." But a repeated need to go overtime reveals a lack of planning and discipline more than it does a passion for content.

It is demoralizing when a class session fizzles out with you desperately raising your voice to add "just one more point" while students bang their binders shut and gather their backpacks. Nor is it optimal to end a class with: "Well, time's up. We'll carry on with this section next time."

We all know what it feels like to bring a class to a firm conclusion just before the clock says we should, in a controlled and lively way. Students are not yet fixated on their next commitments, and there is a sense in the room that the session has been an integrated whole. Finishing early also allows students to approach you and continue the discussion. It is extremely gratifying at the end of a class to have students debating the issues as they leave the room, either with each other or with you. You will more likely create that magic if you end your class a moment early. Most undergraduates today are extremely busy. They may love your class, but that does not mean they have time to sit in it any longer than scheduled.

A class is an event and should end on an upbeat note. How do you orchestrate that? By making each session well-organized, informative, and engaging, by keeping an eye on the clock, and by reserving time at the end for a strong summary and conclusion.

We highly recommend that as part of your planning you decide in advance: "Which one or two sections of content will I leave out if I'm running late?" That way, when the class is almost over, you're not scrambling to bring the ideas to a hasty conclusion. You can avoid this problem by outlining a lecture plan for yourself, complete with time allotments for various sections of the material. Before class, look over your plan carefully and note (directly on the plan) what section can be omitted if you get behind schedule. Then if you find partway through the class that the session is running 10 minutes late, don't panic. Simply skip the 10-minute section you have already identified as expendable, and move into your conclusion on time.

Ending the Course

Just as you want to end each class well, so you want to end the entire course as effectively as possible. We like to reserve a full session at semester's end for review. It gives students the humanizing message that you are not just racing through the curriculum, disseminating as much information as possible. It tells students you have time for questions that will help them understand and enjoy the material. It communicates that you want each of them to do well on the final exam and also to appreciate the fascinating big picture.

The last class session should have a celebratory ambience and should, even more than each individual class, end on a high note. Bring in tea and coffee if you like. Depending on the subject matter, you might choose to end the course dramatically, with a poem or a piece of music that makes a central point. Eleanor sometimes ends her course by having each student shake hands with every other student in the room and offer brief encouraging comments, somewhat like athletes after a game.

We reserve at least 15 minutes at the end of the final class to figuratively step back and give a brief and optimistic overview of the field, to remind students of its many questions that call for exploration, and to recap the value that this discipline can provide for students in any career they might choose. Though we are cautious about encouraging undergraduate students to take further courses in our discipline, which may not be appropriate for some of them, we do invite them to come to us for information, letters of recommendation, or help of any kind. We assure them that we have enjoyed their participation and interest, and urge them to keep in touch. And, as in every individual class throughout the semester, we end a few seconds early and tie up the semester with an articulated farewell to provide closure to the experience we've all had together.

Communication:

Striving for Clarity

Chapter 20

Giving Instructions Effectively

G iving instructions well is intrinsic to good teaching. Whether you are asking students to write a quiz or examine a theory, they will not do it optimally without proper direction. When we find ourselves faced with constant questions of procedure or clarification, we know our instructions have been lacking. "What did you say we should discuss in our small groups?" "When is the term paper due?" "Which lab are we meeting at?" Confusion sometimes stems from students' failing to listen carefully or read handouts. To minimize this, one essential instruction in any course goes something like this: "Read all the handouts carefully, please. You are responsible for knowing the policies stated on them."

However, confusion arises most often when our written or verbal instructions are unclear or inadequate. The best instructions have the following characteristics.

1. They are sequential. "First I'd like you to do this. Then do that. Then do the third thing."

2. They are clearly stated, and difficult to misinterpret. It's best not to get fancy with instructions, but to state them simply. Leave the intellectual challenge for the academic material. It

can also be useful to repeat instructions, or ask if there are any questions about them.

3. They are stated confidently. Try to minimize the use of the question-word "okay?" as in: "I'd really like you to have your project proposals in by this Friday, okay?" It makes instructions sound tentative and uncertain.

4. They are detailed. A common mistake is to make instructions too sketchy, and insufficiently specific. Many instructors are reluctant to give comprehensive directions, partly to avoid seeming patronizing to adult learners and partly because they feel students should have latitude within which to work. But far from being constraining, it is liberating for students to be given guidelines within which they can confidently exercise their intellects and imaginations. Assignments, readings, and group activities all function more smoothly if you have given unambiguous and complete instructions. For example, in small-group work, students cannot address a question, no matter how interesting, if they are confused about whom they're supposed to be talking to, for how long, or whether one of them should be taking notes. Help by outlining those mechanics clearly.

Whenever you foresee that you will be giving instructions in class, write them out for yourself beforehand. Then read them from the point of view of a student. Is there any way to misunderstand the instructions? Have you omitted essential steps? If so, clarify and rewrite before class. Details can slip through the cracks unless we think through instructions beforehand, from beginning to end. We may think we don't need to explain something because it is obvious. But it rarely is. So, for example, we might deliver a set of directions as follows:

"Students, we're going to spend the rest of today's session in the theatre. Let's be clear on exactly what we're going to do. First, please take one of these file cards, write your name on it, and note your choice of topic for the improvisational piece you'll be doing next week. Please hand the card to me on your way out. Then, take a short break, and we'll meet in the theatre in 15 minutes. Please sit in the first three rows of the audience. Once we're there, we're going to watch a demonstration of the acting skills we've been discussing. Then, after the demonstration, you will have a chance to practise those skills."

Conducting examinations provides another situation in which instructions need to be particularly clear. Your instructions might include:

- You have 50 minutes to complete the exam.
- Use pencil only, please.
- Write your name on all sheets of paper you use.
- Restroom breaks are permitted (or not permitted).
- Language dictionaries (for example Spanish-English or Chinese-English) are (or are not) allowed.
- Questions of clarification are permitted. Either raise your hand, or come up to the front and ask.

Some instructions can be included in introductory comments at the top of the exam. But others are better posted on the blackboard and repeated verbally. We suggest you get to the exam room early enough to write instructions on the board. Then, before the exam, read them aloud to students. In such situations overstatement is better than understatement. Students are nervous, and clarity necessary.

Before going to the exam, consider sitting in your office and writing the instructions on paper so you don't forget any once you are there. We instructors are sometimes on edge when administering exams, just as students are when taking them. Try to avoid the annoying situation in which you forget to give one or more instructions, and are compelled to interrupt students during the exam to make the forgotten announcement.

Throughout the semester, when a student is confused by instructions you believe are clearly stated in the syllabus, gently ask the student to read the handout again. However, if a number of students ask the same question, that is usually an indication that your instructions were too easily misinterpreted.

In summary, instructions that are sequential, clear, and adequately detailed make our classes run more smoothly. It also frees us to put most of our energy where it belongs—on facilitating learning of the academic material.

Chapter 21

Encouraging Students' Questions

If our courses are going well, students should be asking questions about the concepts and information that are the heart of the material. As instructors we want to encourage those questions and learn to respond to them effectively. To this end, we try to follow a few basic rules.

1. Always take questions seriously.

    Never laugh at a student question. Do not inject humour into your answer unless the joke is obviously not directed at the student. Learners' questions are a glorious mix of highs and lows. Take every inquiry as a genuine attempt at intellectual exploration.

2. Be positive and encouraging.

    Students need to know that their questions are useful ones. The phrase "good question" is occasionally fine, but easy to overuse, and may occasionally make others feel that their questions were less worthy. There are more effective ways of letting students know that you appreciate their queries, such as a simple smile and an enthusiastic answer. It is also useful to develop a repertoire of phrases such as: "That question takes us into an interesting area," or "Yes, you've anticipated what we were going to talk about next."

3. Draw all class members into the question-and-answer exchange.

Especially in large groups, when one person asks a question many classmates are unable to hear it. Before answering, then, repeat the question clearly and audibly for the rest of the group. Otherwise you create an isolated conversation between yourself and a single student, which is uninformative and frustrating for others. Your physical positioning is also important. Instructors commonly make the mistake of moving toward a student who has asked a question. Try to do the opposite. Back away from the questioner as you reply, widening your field of vision to include everyone. As you are speaking, look over the whole room and make eye contact with as many individuals as possible so that you are answering the question for all students, not just for one.

4. Answer as pointedly and briefly as possible.

Most of us enjoy verbal rambling, and increasingly so the longer we have been teaching and the more knowledge we have amassed. However, when a student asks whether the 20th Century was the most violent in history, or whether Rachel Carson's *Silent Spring* started the modern environmental movement, they do not want or need to hear everything we know about the topic. Undergraduate students are generally hoping for straightforward answers to their questions, understanding that these are complex topics. As well, students will only tolerate so many long monologues before we get a bad reputation and they ask fewer questions.

5. Answer questions immediately, if briefly, rather than deflect-
    ing them.

    Students often ask questions that anticipate topics you had
    planned to discuss later in the lecture or the semester. While
    it is tempting to deflect such queries with "I'd rather not
    answer that now. I'll be dealing with the issue later," such
    a response can be deflating for students. Their curiosity is
    piqued, making the moment a fertile one. That's not to say
    you should make a time-consuming digression. But answer
    the question—briefly—when it arises, then add that you will
    explore the issue further at a later time. One exception to this
    general rule occurs when one or more students continually
    interrupt with questions that are truly irrelevant; such cases
    may require that you not only postpone your answer but speak
    to the student(s) after class.

6. Relate questions to the course material, even if they are
    tangential.

    Every question is a learning opportunity related to the material
    you want students to understand. From time to time a student
    will ask a question that is not directly related to the material
    at hand. If it is completely off topic, a simple "Yes," "No," or
    other quick answer may do. If it's complex, "Let's talk about
    it after class" is often more appropriate. It is unnecessary for
    you to respond extensively to every question or comment.
    But sometimes you will want to remind students of how a
    seemingly unrelated question does pertain to course content.
    Some such questions are attempts to make sense of connections
    to other disciplines. For example, a biology instructor may
    describe a phenomenon using different terminology from that
    used in horticulture for the same concept; students will want
    to make sense of this. Cross-disciplinary "a-hahs" should be
    encouraged, because they remind students that education is

continuous and the divisions between academic disciplines artificial. However, the more tangential the question, the less class time it should be given.

7. Ask for comments from other students.

Often a student question has the potential to spark a useful discussion. Say a class member asks: "How could the Vietnam War have continued so long when there was so much popular opposition?" This might be a good opportunity to open the floor for comments. Set the stage, perhaps with: "It's true there was a great deal of opposition. However, there were other factors or realities that prolonged the war. Can anyone cite such a factor in the United States of the 1960s and 1970s? . . . Can anyone else name another?"

8. Avoid embarrassing students who have asked problematic questions.

If the question or comment shows the individual student's lack of awareness or knowledge, be careful when asking for others' input that they don't embarrass the questioner. A student once stated in Eleanor's class: "I don't believe that smoking or drinking during pregnancy is that bad. I have a friend who smoked and drank during her entire pregnancy, and her baby's fine." If you decide to throw this open to discussion (and other students will be itching to comment), moderate the exchange with compassion for the questioner. You might begin with something like: "Interesting point. This is an experience that some people feel they have had. Yet the scientific evidence is clear that smoking and drinking harm a fetus. What are some possible explanations for this apparent contradiction?" In this way you avoid making the questioner feel foolish, while providing an opportunity for other students to raise points. In the example just cited, students might suggest that one exceptional case does not prove a point, that the baby may develop physical or mental problems later which are not yet evident, or that the mother may be denying her baby's deficits.

9. Elicit student questions before class and during breaks.

Many of the best student questions come to us from individuals just before or after class, or during breaks. This is especially true if we demonstrate our availability and interest by circulating through the room. During breaks and before class, we stroll up and down the rows, chatting with students and asking directly for questions or comments. When we receive a question that would be profitably answered for all students, we give the questioner a quick answer privately, then make a point of sharing the question and answer with the whole class during the next portion of the session, as long as the question is one that will not embarrass the individual. "During the break, one student asked an excellent question. I'd like to answer it for all of you. . . ."

10. Encourage students to bring questions to you during office hours.

Office hours are extremely valuable for students who are too shy to ask questions in front of others or whose learning is enhanced by a personal connection with the instructor. Tempting as it is to use office hours for paperwork, an important part of good teaching is letting students know they are more than welcome to bring questions and concerns to you outside of class time. Emphasize the invitation by leaving your door open during office hours. At the same time, do not feel obliged to indulge the occasional student who uses the time mainly for extended conversations.

The questions you receive during office hours are often valuable ones. Some are unusual observations from students who were reluctant to take such risks during class. Others are personally insightful views of the material. Once in a while you will receive a spate of procedural or content-related questions alerting you that your classroom explanation was insufficient and should probably be clarified for everyone in an upcoming session.

Hold office hours that are convenient to all members of your classes, and let them know you are also available by appointment. Some instructors require that all students attend office hours at least once per semester, as a get-to-know-you session or as a check on their individual progress. We find this time-consuming, and believe there are other effective ways to get to know students. These include: (a) introductory file cards that they fill out on the first day, (b) informal conversations with students before and after class sessions, and (c) a comfortable classroom atmosphere in which students feel willing to express ideas and ask questions often.

Despite your efforts to encourage questions, students may not be asking them. If this is the case, begin by examining whether there is anything you may inadvertently be doing with your body language, tone of voice, or choice of words, to dissuade student queries. Then, try some other strategies. For example, consider asking class members to develop questions in small groups, which is less threatening. Try handing out index cards, asking for questions to be written down and handed in. Depending on the subject matter, you can either ask students to sign their names or keep it anonymous. When questions are anonymous, you will receive more daring (and occasionally facetious) queries. When questions are signed, you will receive safer, more serious ones. Either way, encouragement from you will lead students to ask questions and take an active part in their learning.

Chapter 22

Asking Engaging Questions

*In my first year of teaching, I was fascinated by the big
issues, and believed students would be, too. One day in
class I explained that some psychologists claim human
behaviour is completely determined by environmental
factors, and posed a question I believed would ignite
discussion. "So," I asked, "do humans have free will or
do they not?" I thought a dozen hands would shoot into
the air. Instead there was complete silence. —EB*

If you ask students a question and there is no response, you've
probably asked the wrong question. As we all discover in the
classroom, some questions work and others do not. Some
elicit a range of interested or even excited responses, while others
produce blank stares. Asking the right question is one of the most
challenging aspects of teaching. As with other instructional skills,
there is nothing natural about doing this well. It takes attention
and practice to develop effective behaviours and make them
automatic.

To develop participatory classes, we need to ask our students
frequent questions about the course content and establish a
supportive environment in which learners will be eager to respond.
When asking questions of students:

- Show that you're sincere, that your request is not perfunctory, and that you really want to hear their ideas. Look at students, not at your notes. Smile. Cast your gaze around the class, making eye contact with as many individuals as possible. Your body language and facial expression should invite questions, not discourage them.
- Move away from the lectern if you like, to minimize the physical barrier between yourself and students.
- Pause. Don't be afraid of silence. Not only do students need time to think, but for shy individuals, answering even a straightforward question requires that they summon courage. Wait until there are several hands up before beginning to take comments, to give students a few extra seconds of thinking time (unless the discussion is deliberately fast-paced, such as a review.)

One question you will ask frequently is: "Any questions?" When you do, apply the rules above. Give students a second chance when the information is particularly important, or when some points may have been unclear. We often use the following:

Instructor: Any questions or comments? (Pause)
Students: (No response)
Instructor: Are you sure? (Pause)

When the mood feels right we sometimes ham it up a little, with a smile and, "C'mon, I just know there are questions out there that you haven't yet asked," and "All of your questions are valuable ones," and even occasionally a good-natured "I just don't want to continue until I hear at least one question."

When asking procedural questions, phrase them in a form that will elicit the information you need. Rather than "Does everyone have the handouts?" ask "Is there anyone who did not receive a handout?" Instead of "Can everyone see the board?" ask "Is there anyone who can't see the board?" If you're wondering whether students understood a lecture, rather than "Is that clear?" you will get more useful responses with "Would anyone like clarification on that?" Avoid that flawed question "Does everyone understand?" to which no individual student can really respond. Better to ask "Does anyone have any questions or comments?"

Any question that is phrased "Does everyone . . . ?" cannot literally be answered by any one person and violates the principle: Ask students questions they can answer. It is true that individuals usually understand the spirit of your request, but an imprecise question discourages puzzled students from making themselves known. This is especially true after a chorus of "yeses" indicates that many students believe "everyone understands." In such cases, what you want to know is whether there are any individuals in the room who are not clear on the material and who would like you to review. Of course we don't want to embarrass individuals, so we ask the question in various ways. You might consider: "There may be a few of you who would like me to review that. Anyone?" or "This theory is complex. Would some of you like me to go over it once more?"

Types of Questions

Questions about course content can usefully be divided into different types.

1. Convergent (closed-ended) versus divergent (open-ended).

   Convergent questions demand brief and specific answers. Examples include:

   - When was the Ming Dynasty?
   - Who were three major artists associated with the Cubist movement?
   - What is the definition of a rational number?
   - In addition to *The Wealth of Nations*, what other book did Adam Smith write?

In contrast, divergent questions lend themselves to numerous possible answers and to discussion. Examples include:

- What are some of the features that distinguish the music of Debussy from that of Stravinsky?
- The Baltic area has historically been a crossroads of northeastern Europe. What might be some reasons for that?
- What are some of the factors that have hindered women's attempts to achieve employment equity?
- To analyze these chemical compounds, what lab tests might we consider using?

Convergent questions have the reputation of being less worthy than divergent ones. But there are appropriate times for convergent questions. They can be used to warm up a class, to set the stage for more complex questions, or as a quick review. In general, however, divergent questions are more thought-provoking and will probably form the backbone of your interactions with students.

2. Cognitively lower-order versus higher-order.

Every question is pitched at a particular cognitive level from simple to complex. As we discussed in Chapter 4, these can test knowledge, comprehension, application, analysis, synthesis, or evaluation.

You may want to ask most of your questions at high cognitive levels. However, we suggest you pose a series of questions that builds from low to high to determine whether students grasp the basic information, then understand it, then can apply it, then can analyze or evaluate it. An example of a series of questions at increasing levels might be:

- When was the World Trade Organization (WTO) established?
- What were the stated reasons for establishment of the WTO?
- Based on WTO actions regarding dumping and subsidies, what kinds of rules was it likely to establish regarding services and intellectual property?
- In your view, whose interests are most served by the WTO? What data support your ideas?
- Considering recent events, what do you think is the likely future for the WTO?
- Taking an overview, does the WTO appear to have met its stated objectives?

Phrasing Questions Effectively

Effective questions have a number of characteristics. They are specific and focused, they are challenging but not too difficult, and they encourage students to speculate or explore. In short, they are clear, precise, manageable, and inviting. The following are a few ways in which you can improve your questions.

1. When students are speechless in response to a query, try re-phrasing it. Often the question was too broad, an example of which might be: "What were the reasons for the French Revolution?" Hone, focus, and limit to produce a more effective result.

2. Sometimes the question was aimed at too high a level for the group. Perhaps you asked them to analyze the flaws in a software program before they understood the program in the first place. Move down a bit, as you would gear down in a car to climb a hill. Start at a basic level, then build to higher levels of understanding.

3.   Perhaps the question appeared to demand a fully-formed, perfect answer—something students never feel they have. For example, the following question might be overly challenging. "The discovery of the structure of DNA was a scientific milestone. Why?" or "What's the difference between 19th and 20th Century views of historical 'facts'?" Such questions might be fine for a graduate-school seminar but are too daunting for most classroom discussions. Ideally, we ask questions in class that do not intimidate but rather invite exploration.[19] Use words such as speculate, suggest, guess, and the like.

4.   "Why" questions are problematic because they are often vague, too broad, or unfocused. Happily, such questions can be rephrased. Rather than ask "Why is the analysis-of-variance (ANOVA) the correct statistical test to use on these data?" try replacing it with "What are some of the reasons we would choose to use an ANOVA on these data?" If you introduce a question with "Alienation is a notable theme in the 20th Century novel," try following it up not with "Why?" but with "What could be some reasons for that?" or "Can anyone speculate on how that theme might have arisen?" When we want to ask students "Why?" what we often mean is "How?" or "What?"; rephrasing in this way narrows a question to something more manageable.

Questions do not exist in a vacuum. They are part of a discussion among yourself and the students in the class. We need to respond to learners' answers in ways that encourage intellectual investigation. New instructors often respond to students either too harshly ("No, that's wrong") or too permissively (congratulating any and every answer). Ideally we learn a balanced approach, indicating which answers are more useful and which are less so without embarrassing individuals. Even more important, in exploratory discussions we should not attempt to evaluate every comment by every student. Sometimes it is wiser to simply accept each comment and allow the discussion to flow. (See Chapter 25.)

In summary, then, the best questions challenge students but not beyond their capabilities. They are aimed at appropriate cognitive levels. They are designed to elicit a variety of responses. They promote purposeful examination of important issues. They are brief and clearly stated. They are interesting and likely to motivate. And they are asked in the spirit of rigour yet compassion that should characterize all of our teaching.

Chapter 23

Facilitating Purposeful
Discussions

Useful classroom discussion doesn't just happen. To play a productive role in our courses, it must be carefully planned and skilfully guided.

When planning an upcoming class, pinpoint topics you think would be appropriate for discussion. In other words, plan discussions ahead of time. While some will arise unexpectedly from students' questions or comments, most occur because you know they could be useful at particular points of the lecture for stimulating thought and exploring ideas. Perhaps it would be productive for students to discuss the political and social legacy of Martin Luther King, or the influence of Michel Foucault on psychiatry. You might want them to discuss what comparative anatomy tells us about evolution, or whether the public-school system successfully meets its objectives. There are many possible topics, even in your field alone.

Before planning for specific discussions, remind yourself of the purposes of discussion. They include to:

- involve students in the class;
- allow students to delve more deeply into a topic;
- have learners work with the material, such as applying theory to a situation;

- have learners (rather than you) generate ideas;
- encourage students to explore their attitudes and express their opinions;
- allow students to hear a variety of opinions and ideas;
- help learners develop critical and evaluative thinking skills;
- have students practise analytical skills such as making inferences;
- have students make connections between apparently disparate ideas.

Your preparation and organization will include thinking through what you would like to achieve in the discussion. These will include both "content" and "process" objectives. You want students to learn something about the academic material but also to develop skills in listening, debating, and reasoning.

Decide how to start the discussion by formulating a question. Good discussion questions are relevant to the course material, are neither too difficult nor too easy, are clearly stated, have no obvious right answer, stimulate various points of view, and focus on topics students will care about.

Avoid asking the question out of the blue. Put the issue into context. Make sure students have enough background to address the question. Give them sufficient information to stimulate thought, but not so much as to pre-empt their contributions. Tell them enough to stir their interest. Then ask the question. For more on asking effective questions, see Chapter 22.

Once the discussion gets rolling, your task is to manage it well. Like chairing a meeting, facilitation requires that you not control the conversation, but nevertheless manage it. You want the discussion to have some life of its own without your constantly interrupting and controlling the course of thought. On the other hand, you don't want students to go off on tangents that will not be intellectually useful.

Like so much of teaching, leading discussions is a challenge because it requires being attentive to several things at once. You need to be following the intellectual content of the discussion.

But you also need to guide the process actively, by taking the following steps.

1. Ensure that those who want a chance to speak, get one.

    Think before class about the mechanics of turn-taking. Will you allow students to call out? Or should they somehow indicate their desire to speak, and have you recognize them? Some instructors feel that asking adult students to "put up their hands" is demeaning; they therefore encourage students to call out or just break into the discussion when there is a pause. We advise against it; in such a system only the most assertive get their say. Furthermore, such a procedure inhibits students' listening to each other, because they're too busy waiting for an opportunity to jump in. We suggest, in fact, that in a discussion of any length you keep a speakers' list. When students indicate their desire to speak, jot down their names and take their comments in turn. That way, students can relax and listen, knowing they will get their chance.

2. See that speakers stay brief and on-topic.

    Keep up the pace of the discussion by reining in ramblers who either speak too long or wander off-topic. Make liberal use of eye contact, facial expressions, and hand gestures, to encourage speakers to wrap it up before they have gone on too long. If necessary, insert yourself (interrupting gently) to bring the class back to the topic at hand and remind students of the central issues.

3. Manage the discussion so a few individual students do not dominate.

    Some dominators really do have valuable comments to make, while others say very little of use. Either way, it is important to manage their behaviour or the rest of the class will resent it.

Dealing with dominators is closely related to the general challenge of attaining balanced participation. One step we take, on the very first day of the semester, is to give a pep-talk on the subject. First, remind students how important their involvement is to their own learning. Then, consider saying something like: "Students, we all want to participate effectively in a class. Each of us has a challenge in this regard. For some of you, the challenge will be to speak at all, because you're too shy to express your opinions. For others, who find it easy to speak in groups, your challenge is to be sensitive to the needs of others and not to contribute too often or too long. In our discussions I'll hope to hear from everybody, and see that we're taking others' needs into account as we express our opinions." It's surprising how effective such words can be. Students will appreciate your candor and your concern for everyone in the class.

To deal with dominators moment-to-moment in class, consider the following options. Don't call on them to speak every time their hands are up. Develop a repertoire of useful phrases, such as: "May we hear from someone who hasn't had a chance to comment?" or "Thank you for your ideas, but we need to move on now." And learn to cut off speakers diplomatically in mid-monologue. They do have to breathe sometime.

If a few talkative group members continue to provoke animosity, address them privately after class. We try to be direct but compassionate: "Gerry, you have valuable contributions to make in this class. And we want to hear from you. But I have a responsibility to all students, and probably can't ask for your comments more than a few times per session. I hope you won't be disappointed. We really appreciate your insights."

4.   Provide shy students with opportunities to speak.

The first-day pep-talk described above will encourage reluctant students to comment. However, if many class members are still hesitant to volunteer, you can try other tactics. Ask students to give a comment or opinion to their partner(s) in a group of two or three, or write a question for you on a piece of paper. This can relax learners and give them the confidence to speak out loud later. From time to time you might shake things up by giving students a few moments to leave their seats and sit down with one or two people they don't know to discuss a particular question. Difficult as it is for them, shy students particularly benefit from being required to meet new people.

In general (unless you are skilled in the use of Socratic method) we do not advise putting students on the spot by calling on them when they have not volunteered. But occasionally you know that an individual has a valuable opinion or observation because s/he has told you privately or expressed it in an assignment. In such cases, you might risk: "Sally, you found some interesting results when you investigated this question. Would you like to mention what you found?" or "Leonard, you've started your own small business. Could you tell us how you handled this problem?"

5.   Ensure that a variety of opinions is expressed.

The most valuable discussions are those which generate a range of opinions. If everyone expresses the same ideas, the discussion doesn't go very far. Unfortunately, once a given point of view has been expressed, other students are sometimes hesitant to contradict. We often find the following line successful for pulling a discussion out of a rut: "Does anyone have another opinion?" or "Probably some people in this room feel differently about the issue. May we hear an alternative 'take' on this controversy?" Develop your own versions of this question, which gives students permission to express a mix of viewpoints. Also important is to be as supportive as possible to student comments and questions, which sends a message of open-mindedness and acceptance. Never be derisive of any student comment.

6. Provide stimulation when the discussion needs a boost.

    Step in occasionally when you feel students have exhausted a topic, have gone off track, or are momentarily stuck. Step in as well to clarify when there is confusion, sometimes because different participants are talking about different parts of a problem. You might narrow the discussion, which sometimes provides focus, for example: "We're talking about a number of different factors affecting urban land prices. Perhaps for a moment we should zero in on 'supply' as a factor." You can briefly summarize what has been said, to remind participants of points they wanted to make. Or you can ask another question that will usher participants in a potentially productive direction.

7. Focus and steer the discussion so it goes somewhere.

    Say you are giving a class on environmental law, centred on the toxic-waste contamination of Love Canal in New York in the 1970s. Students have read about the case, and you would like them to discuss whether Love Canal could occur today. If you choose to open broadly by asking for reasons for the poisoning of Love Canal, you will get a wide range of answers. "Hooker Chemical dumped its toxic waste there," or "There were too few environmental regulations at that time," or "The free-enterprise system encourages this kind of waste disposal—corporations do anything they can get away with," or "Back then, residents in the area were too trusting of the company." Such a barrage of responses can be a stimulating start to a discussion and remind students that large problems do not have single causes or simple solutions. But academically, this discussion will only be useful if you help students focus.

    How do you make sense of disparate ideas? Categorization is one strategy. If you've scribbled all the ideas on the blackboard or overhead, consider looking over the list and suggesting that ideas be grouped. "I see a number of different actors in this scenario. First, there's the company. What did it do to contribute to the problem? Then there's the government. How did it contribute? Then there are local residents. Can they be said to have contributed to the problem? And then there are the larger actors of society itself or the system which helped allow this to occur."

You can then zero in on any of these categories, tying them into issues of environmental law. You might nudge students toward thinking about the effects of tighter environmental regulations on the behaviour of various actors. Or you might hone in on 1970s environmental laws, and compare them with environmental regulations of today, to explore whether Love Canal could legally occur again. However you want to proceed, useful discussions require focus so students feel they have accomplished something at the close.

8. Listen well, and respond to students' comments when appropriate.

    Model good listening for other students. Make eye contact with each speaker and demonstrate that you have heard what s/he said. Comment when you feel it would be useful. Some contributions may demand context, or may be so insightful or so problematic that you feel the need to say so. However, it is not necessary to respond to every statement. That said, occasionally summarizing a student's comment can encourage understanding and response. So: "Charlie, I think you're suggesting that American television does not accurately portray the immigrant experience, that it makes life for minorities look rosier than it really is. Is that what you mean? What do other people in the class think about this?"

9. Manage the time, and wrap up discussions before they fizzle out.

    If you have allocated 10 minutes for discussion, and have two questions for students to address, do not let discussion of the first question extend for nine minutes. Once you spark a discussion, especially if students are participating enthusiastically, you will be tempted to allow it to go on too long. It is gratifying watching students exchange ideas on the important issues you have raised. Still, discussion uses valuable class time. And your students do not need to have said the last word on the subject. Better to leave them with a few lingering thoughts and questions rather than wring the topic dry. As well, students sometimes complain that they didn't come to university to spend hours in the classroom listening to peers whose opinions they could access in the cafeteria. They came to hear experts give accurate information and well-founded opinions. They have a point: Keep discussions moving and—unless it's a seminar course—do not let them take over the class.

10. Give students something to take home from the discussion.

Too often participants exchange valuable ideas, but later have trouble remembering what those were. When a discussion has gone on for some minutes, students will often forget even the most important points that were made. To enhance the pedagogical value of a discussion: summarize the main points yourself; ask students to do so either in small-group conversation or on paper; or brainstorm the main points with the whole class. Any such technique allows students to take notes and re-read them later, thereby gleaning more from the discussion in the long term.

Chapter 24

Physical Movement
and Voice

Our bodies and our voices are the instruments through which our teaching is accomplished. Most of us are academics with little training in the physical and dramatic arts. Yet our teaching will be better if we think about how best to use our physical selves in the process of imparting information. This requires energy and effort, which we can only devote if we know our material and are well-prepared for class.

In using your voice, clarity is a primary goal. Clarity requires that you speak comprehensibly in a number of ways:

- loudly enough for all students to hear;
- slowly enough for listeners to understand;
- pronounced or enunciated articulately;
- employing vocabulary that is college-level but not beyond the majority of students in the room.

Most of us do not use our voices as effectively as we might. We cling to a narrow range of volume, tempo, and pitch. We fall into habits of speech that to others sound uninteresting or even monotone. We may be excited about our course material, but if that excitement does not manifest in some detectable way, students won't know it. Fortunately, even slight variations in voice can give conversation excitement and infuse our lectures with life. Varying the voice is one of the quickest and easiest ways to improve teaching.

Try consciously to alter the basic elements of voice, and to inject expressiveness into your speech. Listen to yourself and notice whether you vary your pitch. In speaking, as in singing, we provide interest to listeners by moving up and down a pitch scale. Even just a little variety makes a difference. Then, occasionally vary the volume. From time to time it is appropriate to raise the voice or lower it to a whisper, for emphasis or to make an emotional or moving point.

From time to time, play with the tempo or speed at which you speak. We suggest you generally speak at a moderate pace, avoiding the common presenter's trap of racing through the material. But that said, the occasional sentence spoken either quickly or almost painfully slowly, or an emphatic pause, can be dramatic and memorable.

Actors learn to vary volume, pitch, and tempo through exaggeration and experimentation; instructors can as well. Consider trying out the range of your voice in an empty classroom or in front of the mirror at home. When experimenting with no-one else around, try shouting more loudly and whispering more softly than you ever would in a real situation. This will help you find the limits of your voice and build confidence in a range of possibilities. Daring to use your voice imaginatively can inject variety and interest into your lectures, and increase your enjoyment and professional effectiveness.

Physical Movement

There are several ways we can use physical movement to improve our teaching. One of these is to use gestures. Don't be afraid to move your hands and arms to make a point, as you would sitting in your living room with friends or playing a game of charades. Instructors should be their enthusiastic selves. There's nothing unprofessional about it.

Plenty of eye contact also helps. Try to make eye contact with a wide range of students—every one if possible—not just the few who ask questions most often or who nod and smile a lot. Scan the classroom constantly, seeing as many people as you can. Keep your eyes moving. Watch students at the sides and at the back of the room, not just those in the middle and at the front. Any one of those students, even the quiet ones, may potentially have his or her life changed by your class, and every one deserves attention. There are two other reasons not to limit eye contact to only a few students. It can create the impression in the class that you have favourites. It can also encourage one or more students to develop crushes on you or to feel that you will give them special treatment.

When you speak, look directly at the class as much as possible rather than at inanimate objects such as your notes, the overhead projector, the video machine, or the chalkboard. If you use the chalkboard or flip charts extensively, this presents a particular challenge based on the physical positioning of the board. Even experienced instructors often inadvertently commit the error of speaking to the board, with their backs to the class, so students can't hear and do not feel included. There are two ways to handle this problem:

1. If you do speak while writing on the chalkboard, develop the technique of writing while turning your body as much as possible to face the class. Most experienced elementary or high-school teachers have mastered this. It's similar to the acting technique in which two characters in a play speak to each other while standing with their bodies facing the audience. It just takes a little practice. Try it in an empty classroom, using various positions, and see what works best for you.

2. Simply do not speak while writing on the board. Constant speaking is unnecessary; sometimes a few seconds of silence is best while students copy equations or lists into their notes. You can also glance back and forth from board to students, to

maintain the contact. When you have finished writing, turn to face the class again and resume your verbal explanation.

Being aware of your physical positioning in the classroom will also enhance your teaching. As you stand and move around, everyone should be able to see you at all times, and you should be able to monitor the whole class. (See Chapter 27.) Try to avoid, therefore, standing in the middle of the group. By all means move around the room. But place yourself on the side or in a corner where you can see and be seen by everyone. Positioning yourself for maximum possible interaction with students will keep you in touch with their needs and allow you to provide a high-quality class.

Chapter 25

Giving Beneficial Feedback

Feedback includes observations, comments, and suggestions that you make in either oral or written form to students about their work. "Maya, this paper is well-outlined and organized. However, it could have a stronger conclusion." "Rosa, your insight helps us explain the central problem here." "Raj, your answer touches on an important point, but doesn't quite address the main issue."

As instructors we are more effective in this aspect of the work if we remember four basic characteristics of useful feedback. Good feedback is:

- immediate,
- positive,
- specific,
- focused on the behaviour, not the individual.

1. Good feedback is immediate.

When we give feedback to students in classroom discussion, the feedback is always immediate. "Yes, you've pointed out George Orwell's experience in the Spanish Civil War in shaping his strong opposition to totalitarianism. But can you say more about the political sentiments behind his *Nineteen Eighty-Four?*"

When we give feedback to students on written work it is, by definition, after the fact. The simple rule here is: Try to return students' papers, term projects, and exams—complete with written comments—as soon as possible. Keeping up with marking is one of the most difficult aspects of teaching. Sometimes our workload is such that we are unable to return students' papers for days or even weeks. When this happens, they survive. But students derive the most benefit when the feedback occurs soon after the work is done. The assignment is fresher in their minds, and they have more opportunity to apply your suggestions throughout the rest of the course. They're much happier that way, too.

2. Good feedback is as positive as possible.

Open your feedback by outlining a strength of the comment, the paper, or the presentation. "Scott, you've described in detail why proportional representation might be a useful alternative to our current electoral system. And you've carefully pointed out drawbacks of the present system."

It is easy to give positive feedback to students who excel. But even low-quality student work has kernels of the admirable in it. If a term paper is convoluted and disorganized, that may mean the student got lost in a sea of academic literature but that s/he did struggle to do the research, albeit misguidedly. How about: "Jen, you've done a lot of research and obviously spent time on this. I appreciate the effort. However . . ." Needless to say, all positive feedback should be genuine.

Academics get so accustomed to honing in on imperfections, they often neglect to see the effort, the organization, and the beauty in a student's work. Initiate your comments by acknowledging the work that has been done. Even though the student knows there's a "However . . ." coming, your acknowledgment of their effort makes them more amenable to suggestions. As well, your feedback is intended not only to encourage students to change some qualities of their work, but to help them identify and retain those qualities that are laudable. Recognizing their strengths may be every bit as important as understanding what needs to be improved. If a student does not know what he did well, he may not do it again next time.

We cannot over-emphasize the value of positive feedback as a powerful force in motivating learners. Like all of us, students need to know that their labours are productive and appreciated. In commenting on students' papers, we suggest you close with: Main Strengths: _____; Suggestions: _____. Using a word like "suggestions" rather than "weaknesses" allows you to emphasize the positive and give pointers without sounding overly critical. It also focuses on the future rather than the past.

3. Good feedback is specific.

This is one of the most useful communication skills we have ever learned. Whether you are admiring a child's crayon drawing, giving a performance review to an executive vice-president, or commenting on an undergraduate's thesis, be as specific as possible both in your praise and in your suggestions.

Unless followed immediately by more explicit comments, the following are not very helpful: "Good work." "This thesis is top-notch." "This paper is not of university quality." "Your presentation was poor." Such comments give students no indication that you actually read and thought about their work, no information on what they did right or wrong, and no suggestions on how to improve their work in the future. The best feedback is genuinely useful to the individual.

"Marnie, in your paper on special-needs education you have summarized the arguments thoroughly and in your own words, demonstrating that you understood it. You argued that students with special needs have mixed experiences in the mainstream school system, and cited evidence. Your main evidence was compelling because of its emotional appeal, but was it really an example of systemic problems? As well, your writing needs a little work: note my markings on grammatical errors. Overall, however, a good paper."

"David, your presentation was fascinating in its depth of exploration of the emotional lives of seniors. Your videotaped interviews with nursing-home residents were moving, and humanized the elderly. They were also full of information about the range of emotions that people continue to feel in their senior years. Technically, the videos were professionally done in details such as focus and lighting. Next time, try to keep any video to five minutes as requested. As well, try to end with a conclusion or an obvious wrap-up."

The more specific your comments, the more meaningful they are, and the more useful for shaping the learning process.

4.   Useful feedback focuses on the behaviour, not the individual.

This insight applies in many situations other than teaching—for example, in child-rearing, in which we want to shape actions and attitudes without making a child feel bad. Behaviour is easier to change than personality. Good feedback, therefore, zeros in on the work, not the student. Whether the answer is "good" or "bad," "right" or "wrong," direct your comments to what the student did, not to who s/he is as a person. So instead of "Amy, you're wrong on that one," much better to say "Amy, that suggestion doesn't quite address the main problem. Could we come at the issue from another angle?"

As for written comments in the margins of students' papers, try to apply the same concept. So, for example, avoid criticisms that could seem to a sensitive student as if they were directed at him/her rather than at the paper. Put yourself in the student's place and try to imagine how a particular comment might feel. We also recommend that you use pencil, not pen. This practice allows you to erase and change a comment if you feel on reflection that it was too harsh or otherwise not quite right. Remember that students take professors' remarks very seriously. As well, pencilled notes are less obtrusive and less likely to seem disrespectful. When we were university students, having instructors hand back papers covered in red ink was demoralizing, even if numerous of the comments were positive. Some instructors word-process their comments and attach them to the students' work. This can also save time, since most of us type more quickly than we write.

While students appreciate feedback on their written work, they do not need constant assessment of their oral contributions. So, in class discussions it is not always desirable to evaluate every student comment. Instead it can be useful to simply listen, nod to show that you heard, and allow the discussion to proceed naturally. This practice emerges from the psychotherapeutic techniques of Carl Rogers.[20] The simplest Rogerian technique is to indicate with facial expression or body language and perhaps a word or two that you heard and appreciate the comment, but to give no evaluative feedback on its content. Another technique is to reword or paraphrase the student's comment to show that you understood it or ensure that they said what they really meant to say. If a student comments, "Sartre is obsessed with whether life has meaning. That's the main issue in his writings," you might respond: "So it seems to you that no matter what topic he appears to be discussing, Sartre is actually exploring ultimate meaning or purpose." Paraphrasing has a number of advantages. It demonstrates that you are listening carefully to what students have to say. It increases clarity in discussions by helping speakers be precise (they'll let you know if you misunderstood them) and ensuring that other students understood the speakers' ideas. Non-evaluative feedback also liberates students to make comments and explore ideas without worrying about whether or not you will approve.

Seeking Student Feedback

It is useful to obtain regular student feedback on your teaching and on your class. This is especially the case in the first few years as teachers are developing their own instructional styles. Student feedback serves two purposes. It acts as a confidence booster by letting you know you are on the right track, and also provides ideas for what you might improve. Student feedback continues to be important as we mature in the profession. Students talk about us whether we like it or not. It is helpful to know what they are saying.

We recommend that you seek student feedback informally, perhaps once per semester, with a short anonymous questionnaire asking about any categories that are important to you, such as:

- Content (Too complex or about right? Suggestions for topics of interest?)
- Workload (Too much, too little, or about right?)
- Organization and communication (Well-organized? Clear or unclear?)
- Teaching style (Respectful? Encouraging? Sufficiently or insufficiently varied?)

Ensure that such questionnaires are brief and clearly worded, with sufficient space for student comments. As you're handing out the questionnaires, you can also verbally encourage their written suggestions, demonstrating that you understand the value of useful feedback.

Management:

Developing Techniques for Smoothly Functioning Classes

Chapter 26

Managing your Physical Space and Materials

There are a number of aspects of physical space and materials that must run smoothly if our classes are to do so.

First is the classroom itself. It is possible to run a good session even in a bad classroom. If the physical space is dark and dingy, too big or too small, messy, or ill-equipped, you can transcend these limitations with your enthusiasm and organization. However, creating great learning experiences will be easier if you start with an appropriate space. You may find that you have more choice of classrooms than you think if you speak with your campus room-booking officials.

The best room is the right size. Ideally, whether your student enrolment is 10 or 500, the classroom is just large enough to accommodate everyone. That ensures that students will be seated close to each other, creating a critical mass that does not exist when people are dotted around a cavernous area. Little depletes the energy in a group like a lot of empty seats and unused space. If you are assigned a classroom that is much too large, consider roping-off the back section or otherwise requiring students to sit closer to the front and to each other. This is particularly important for participatory exercises in which you want students to speak with each other. Mere proximity encourages interaction and makes small-group work more natural.

The optimal classroom is one with movable chairs so students can easily break into pairs or small groups. If you have a small class of less than 50 people and the luxury of movable chairs, consider shuffling seats and tables into semicircles. If you teach in rooms with fixed seating, don't despair. Many instructors create a lively and cooperative atmosphere in such rooms. With really large rooms you can number the rows from front to back: 1, 2, 1, 2, 1, 2 . . . either by running up the aisle yourself and calling out numbers (students love it), or with any other system you can imagine. Once each student knows whether s/he is in Row 1 or Row 2, ask all students in Rows 1 to turn around to Rows 2 and meet one or two students. Ask them to form groups of three to four, give them a question to discuss, and you've got immediate group-work even in very large lecture halls.

Before the semester begins, visit the classroom you have been assigned. Spend some time there. Note the configuration of chairs, desks, and equipment, and ask yourself how these can accommodate your needs. Determine whether you will want to make rearrangements before your class sessions. Hopefully you will not need major furniture and equipment overhauls, especially if the classroom is occupied until a few minutes before your class begins each week.

Before each session, get to the classroom early so you can organize the space and your physical materials. You will want to be sure that tables and chairs are arranged optimally, and that chalkboards are erased. Yes, previous instructors should have done that, but sometimes they don't. Most critically, you will want to be sure that your equipment is in place and operational. Check all machines before class, or they will not work during! Never start a class without making sure the overhead projector, TV/VCR, laptop computer, or other piece of equipment, is functioning. This includes low technology; if you plan to use the boards, make sure there is chalk and a brush. If you use an overhead projector, find out what to do if the bulb burns out. Know how to install a new bulb and make sure you have one on hand. Many modern overhead projectors are equipped with two bulbs. Check before every class to make sure both are working.

Think through in advance how you will manage if an overhead machine or other piece of equipment fails. Your classroom may have a telephone hot line to the audio-visual department that sends someone running to fix technical problems. If not, will you abandon the activity and carry on with it next time? If you do forego the planned exercise, you will need a substitute activity. Alternatively, you might continue the activity in a modified form. Being mentally prepared for these small emergencies makes us better able to cope when they occur.

Make sure videos are cued up and ready to go. Avoid the mortifying situation of trying to find the starting point of your video segment while 5 or 105 people are staring at you. This may sound self-evident, but most of us have made the mistake of thinking our video was cued up, only to realize during class that it was not. The best learning sessions are those that flow seamlessly from your pointed lecture directly into a brief video, which naturally inspires a discussion. Try not to hamper the flow by having a tussle with a machine.

For good teaching, your paper system has to be well-organized. I like to have at least three different piles of stuff in front of me when I teach. One is my lecture plan. The second is any supporting materials I might need. The third is my overheads. —HR

Have your lecture notes and overhead transparencies in neat piles, in the order in which you plan to move through them. Transparencies are best handled if they are in cardboard frames or in three-ring binders, or with sticky labels for identification— in some arrangement that allows you to get at them quickly. It doesn't matter which system you choose, but try to have one.

If you are teaching with the aid of a laptop, make sure the machine is up and running before class starts. If you are planning to pull up web-sites in class and project these on a screen, check out the sites beforehand to make sure they are accessible and that the sites serve the pedagogical function you think they do. Consider bookmarking them for speedy access.

When writing on the board, make equations, words, or sketches large and readable. No matter which technology you are employing, "write big" so students can see the information easily. If you prepare overheads before class, we recommend using very large type. It focuses students' attention, and avoids the common problem in which students are so busy trying to read the overhead that they cannot concentrate on the academic material. The form should always facilitate, not interfere with, the content of your classes.

Chapter 27

Discouraging Disruptive Behaviour

*In my first year of teaching a college course, I had
constant problems with a few talkers who would laugh
and whisper at the back of the classroom. I was horrified
to find this behaviour at university, was unprepared to
deal with it, and failed miserably. My attempts to quiet the
talkers were timid extensions of my beginner's insecurity,
and the whispering continued, interfering with the work
and enjoyment for everyone else in the class* —FB

There is little that is more frustrating to serious university students than the instructor who allows persistent talking and other disruptions during class. The vast majority of students are attentive, polite, and interested. However, a few distracting students affect them all. Some groups do seem innately talkative and can be difficult to control, but if constant interruptions are occurring then we as instructors are doing something wrong.

We need to be in control of our classes without being unreasonable or inflexible. We need to create environments that are congenial and inviting but rigorous. We need to plan classes that are organized, interesting, and well-paced. We need to provide students with structured opportunities in class to speak and discuss the material so they won't feel the need to whisper furtive comments. And we need to project a strong message that random talking, laughing, and the like are not tolerated. Experienced instructors know to set this tone early in the semester. Relaxing the rules later is easy, tightening them is difficult.

The first ingredient in developing a controlled class is attitude. Our attitudes should be based on compassion and respect—for ourselves, for all students, and for the learning enterprise in which the class is engaged. Compassion for ourselves recognizes that our teaching should not be debased by student rudeness or inattentiveness. Compassion for students recognizes that most of the class should not suffer for the disruptions of a few. Compassion for the small number of problem students recognizes that they need behavioural boundaries.

We all seek to develop open and lively classes that encourage interaction relevant to the material, and appreciate the occasional joke. However, while students are enjoying your class, they should also be working hard. They should want to attend your class for what they learn there, not just for entertainment. Your goal, then, is to develop a course that is enjoyable but full of challenge, where students feel safe to express themselves but with the good of other classmates in mind. Many students have to make sacrifices to earn the money to attend college, and their primary objective is to learn what they need to realize their goals.

Once you feel secure in this attitude, the second step in developing a controlled class requires that you use specific management skills.

1. Get students' attention.

    Do not start speaking, at the beginning of the class or after any activity, until you have everyone's attention. Failing to wait for silence gives the message that you don't mind students talking while you speak, and that what you have to say is not important. Beginning to speak before the group is attentive also means you will be asked to repeat what you said. Instructors sometimes begin class without drawing the group to attention because they feel it is patronizing to adults to do so. But this is not about power, control, or authority. It is about common politeness and learning effectiveness.

Instructors sometimes neglect to get students' attention because they simply do not know how. New instructors dread the prospect of attempting to secure the attention of the class and having students ignore them and continue to chat. We recommend that you develop a few basic techniques to draw the group together. It could be as simple as two or three hand-claps, or a wave of the hand as you stand obviously ready to begin. Or simply: "All right, it's time to begin," then wait until everyone is ready. Some instructors use the intense "teacher's stare" that most public-school teachers have in their survival kits. Looking at individual talkers for a moment usually does the trick. If a few students persist in chatting, stroll toward them: proximity works like magic.

2. Develop effective pacing.

Come to class prepared and ready to facilitate a well-paced class session. From the start of a session until the end, keep the class upbeat and moving, which will sustain students' interest. Like a radio announcer, avoid lengthy gaps except when you have asked a question and want to give students time to think. The orchestration or choreographing of the class should be such that the pace of lecture and activities is smooth, with a little variation for emphasis from time to time—some pauses for effect, or a little humour. Performance should never take precedence over content, but our students learn most when we present material in ways that hold their interest.

The pace of the class does not always have to be fast, depending on the complexity of the course material. You probably wouldn't rush through an explanation of Rousseau's concept of the social contract. But the class itself should not drag, and should feel at every moment that it is going somewhere. This is especially important in groups that tend to be talkative and that must therefore be managed more closely than others. To achieve good pacing, know your academic material. Then have the material carefully planned and well-ordered, complete with examples, so you're not searching for ideas during class. As in chess where the best defence is a good offence, the best way to avoid management problems is to be confident and well-organized.

3. Plan for transitions.

Prepare smooth transitions for switching from one topic or activity to another. Transitions are a danger point in every class. It is when you are fumbling, shuffling with papers, or figuring out what to do next, that students begin to flip through books and make comments to each other.

Have your physical materials organized and set to go. As discussed in the previous chapter, make sure you have checked out the VCR, the computer, or the overhead projector, to ensure it works when you want it to. See that papers, overhead transparencies, and other materials are ordered and handy. We have all had the unhappy experience in which the VCR refuses to function, or we can't find the next transparency or the articles we intended to pass around. The instant that happens, even with adult learners, students start to talk among themselves and the flow of the class is interrupted.

When you're teaching, there's no rest. While bringing one piece of material to conclusion, you are already thinking one step ahead about what's coming next. That's why you need to know the material so well and be confident in how you've organized it, because only part of your brain can be on the content. The rest has to be concerned with the presentation itself. I like to have transitions planned in advance, and be present enough that I can move right into the next activity without pausing, and switch topics without shuffling notes. —HR

4. Choose the right level of difficulty.

Make sure you are pitching the material at a high enough level to hold the interest of the majority of students. One of the challenges in teaching at college and university is that our classes often have huge ranges in intellectual ability and grounding in the discipline. Make sure you're not boring students by aiming lectures at the lowest common denominator. Neither should you speak only to the few extraordinary members of the group. Try directing your lecture at about the 75th percentile, so the bright students are included and others are challenged but not lost.

You will find at times that some of your students have abundant background in the course material while others have none. If the course has been represented as Introductory, then your responsibility is to the neophytes. If it has been billed as Advanced, your responsibility is to the advanced students; beginners should be directed to outside readings that will help them catch up. It is unrealistic to think you can start giving students private tutorials in material they were expected to know already. We say this from the experience of having spent hours doing just that in our first years of teaching, motivated by a laudable empathy for students but a lack of understanding of our own time constraints. If you assess students' prior knowledge and find that a large percentage of the class lacks important background, you may have to slightly readjust your schedule and deliver the information during class time. Alternatively, you may offer a one-time background session during a lunch hour or meeting block for students who need it.

5. Monitor classes continuously.

When teaching, scan the room frequently to see whether students need anything—further explanation of a theory, another example of a point, or less detail. Maybe you moved on to Point B before they really understood Point A. You should have an ongoing sense throughout the class of whether students are interested or bored, whether they are with you or not. If you are scanning constantly, you will notice when a student has a query (or even a puzzled look). While you need not interrupt yourself in mid-sentence, you can let the individual know that she has been recognized. So if you're in the middle of making a point and a student puts up a hand, you can acknowledge it ("Rick, I'll take your comment in a minute"), finish your point, then ask for the comment.

Position yourself physically in the classroom so you can see the entire group at all times. Stand at the perimeter of the room, at the front, back, or sides. If you are standing in the middle, there are always some students who can't see your face, and whom you cannot see. You know how frustrating it is in a restaurant when you need a glass of water or an extra spoon, and can't get the attention of a server? Like restaurant serving staff, instructors need to be monitoring the room constantly. If students are discussing an issue or working on a problem in small groups, as you walk around the room place yourself so that you can always view as much of the room and as many individuals as possible. If you join the discussion in one small group, keep an eye on the others so you can move and join any group that is having trouble. In situations such as labs where students are working individually and you are circulating and giving assistance, continue to visually monitor the whole group. Then if a student asks for help while you are momentarily busy with someone else, you can still indicate that you'll be right over. It is reassuring for students to know that help is on the way. During small-group or individual work, your visibility will keep students focused too. Even mature adults have a tendency to stay on task more readily if the instructor is observing.

6. Respond confidently when problems arise.

If one or more students are disruptive, deal with the problem immediately. Look directly at the individuals and make it clear that the behaviour is unacceptable. Eye contact and body language are usually sufficient, though you may have to say a word or two. Try not to embarrass the individuals, but make your attitude unmistakable. If they persist, speak to them privately afterward. Tell them you will ask chronically disruptive students to leave the class. If they continue, though it rarely comes to this, be prepared to follow through and request that thcy leave.

In summary, to develop a well-managcd class, we need a confident attitude and sound teaching skills. Good classroom management is based on the foundation skills of thorough planning and organization. There is little opportunity for restless or unmotivated students to subvert the class if we come prepared with an engaging and informative presentation, if we know our material, if we monitor the room constantly, and if we keep the class moving. In other words, like most aspects of teaching, effective management begins with good planning and organization. Add to that an attitude of respect for ourselves and for students, and we'll experience minimal behavioural problems in the classroom.

Chapter 28

Accommodating Various Learning Styles

Some students learn best by reading information, others by hearing it spoken aloud. Some learn well under pressure and with time limits, others do not. Some must personally experience a three-dimensional demonstration to understand a physical concept; others can extrapolate from words on a page. Some excel on examinations; others tighten up and perform worse than they should, given their knowledge and understanding.

Much has been written in the educational literature about different learning styles, especially in the past few years when classrooms have become more diverse and we are teaching increasingly heterogeneous collections of students. College populations are composed of a wide range of ethnic, cultural, and religious backgrounds, a variety of ages, and of course both women and men. The following are steps we can take to help accommodate today's learners.

1. Get to know your students, and try to link the academic material to their realities.

    If you ask your students on the first day of class to fill out file cards, encourage them to tell you details about their backgrounds, interests, and pursuits. (See Chapter 12.) This will help you speak directly to them, whether by using a sports analogy in explaining a course concept, or demonstrating that you understand the value of certain cultural practices.

2.   Impart information through numerous different modes.

If students are having trouble comprehending principles of light refraction or Darwin's theory of evolution, your explanation may not have spoken to them. Try explaining it anew with a different approach or a fresh example. If they don't understand return on investment with words, try explaining it using tables. If they have trouble envisioning the physiological characteristics of cardiac muscle even with diagrams, try using an analogy to something they've experienced. Bring in a three-dimensional model. Try visual approaches. Try novel verbal ones. Be dramatic. Do whatever works to help students understand.

3.   Evaluate students using a variety of methods.

Allow students to play to their different strengths by offering various question types on exams and even graphic or oral means of communicating ideas, if that is appropriate for your course. Assignments give even more leeway for creative methodology. While writing assignments are valuable and often used, there are a number of other possible options for assignments. (See Chapter 8.)

4.   Remember that some students are not comfortable expressing opinions in class.

If a few students are not contributing to discussions it may be because their age or their family, ethnic, or cultural backgrounds make it difficult for them to voice personal opinions or speak in public. Develop phrases that might draw out reluctant students. We use: "May I hear from someone who hasn't had a chance to speak yet?" "Perhaps there's a different point of view in the room," and "I'm sure someone here has had another experience."

Consider giving students less-vulnerable ways to participate. Asking individuals to speak in small groups is relatively unthreatening and will usually elicit the cooperation of even the most reserved. As well, you can ask students to write comments and questions on paper that they hand in to you. (See Chapter 13.) You might also consider outside participation strategies including student discussion groups and Internet conference forums. (See Chapter 31.)

5. Widen the curriculum to include students of all cultural backgrounds.

Teaching a multicultural group is a challenge. References that you might have assumed students would understand—from hockey to Disney—may not make the point with students raised in other cultures. Keep an eye out for aspects of the curriculum that are exceedingly ethnocentric and that you might be able to restate in more inclusive ways. You might also consider making reference to specific cultural variants either as examples in making a point, or as a whole component of content. Whether teaching architecture or film, you can occasionally make points by using examples from other countries represented in the classroom. You will want to do so in a way that is sensitive and doesn't single out students but rather makes them feel included. In courses on politics or zoology, you might ask students to offer international examples. Rather than ask on the spot, give them time to collect their thoughts. Or, when teaching music, ask a few students (privately in advance) whether they would like to contribute a song from their own cultures. In courses on human biology, you might mention that traditional Chinese medicine has a whole complex system—different from that of Western medicine—of looking at bodily energy and function. When teaching psychology, you can open up discussion of a different world view by introducing students to the concept of the Medicine Wheel, a holistic aboriginal approach to life.

6. Recognize the special character of older students.

Today's college classes often have at least a few students in their 30s, 40s, and beyond. Variously called mature, returning, or simply older students, they may possess considerable life and work experience that gives them practical insights into the theoretical material of the course. Older students are often highly motivated and successful. They tend to have a confidence that younger students do not possess. And because they are closer to your age (sometimes older), they frequently have a more relaxed relationship with the instructor. For these reasons, such students can contribute generously to class discussions, and their contributions should be encouraged.

However, mature class members sometimes contribute too heavily, in the opinion of younger students. If older students control classroom discussion, deal with the situation as you would with students of any age. Consider giving a start-of-semester pep-talk, emphasizing that effective classroom participation means contributing to, but not dominating, discussions. Then, during the semester, develop your own kind but firm strategies such as those outlined in Chapter 23. Your responsibility is to all class members, not just to a few. Any individual students' past experiences, while interesting, are not always representative.

You might also consider ways to access older students' life experience appropriately in the classroom, perhaps in special presentations. Or you may suggest that such students form study groups as outlets for their many ideas.

7. Treat all students as important.

Try to ensure that you are not showing preferences for certain students. When you converse casually with students before or after class sessions, be careful not to give attention only to those whose particular traits—age, ethnicity, gender, obvious interest in your discipline, or other personal characteristics—provide you with easy common ground. Attempt to divide your attentions equally among students, and demonstrate that every one of them is important to you.

Chapter 29

Helping Students Take Notes to Get the Most from Class

When we feel organized, it contributes to our confidence and ease of management of class sessions. When students feel organized, it contributes to their feeling that the class is a cooperative enterprise, and fewer classroom-management problems arise. One important way for both instructors and students to feel organized is for you to give students an outline and background to the lecture that will help them take useful notes. As with any aspect of teaching, you should plan how you will facilitate this before the start of your course.

Most of us remember, as undergraduates, attending lectures that consisted of 50 minutes of monologue while we scribbled as much into our notes as possible. Today, as instructors, many of us would prefer a more organized system as well as a more interactive one.

Good lectures have an obvious structure which learners can follow. Such sessions require that students be involved and take notes, but not spend all their energy writing. If students are scrambling to write down every word, they're not thinking and will not be able to ensure the information is clear to them, let alone ask penetrating questions. We are reminded of the widely-quoted and humorous description of lectures as "events in which information passes from the notes of the professor to the notes of the students without passing through the minds of either." Ideally, students' main activity is listening rather than writing. If they concentrate on what you are saying, they can then comment, question, and challenge.

However, students also need notes to take away from a class. They want a record of what occurred in order to study for final exams, since good notes stimulate the memory. Students also feel more secure that something important unfolded in the classroom when they leave with a few pages of writings.

You have several choices for helping students follow the lecture and take notes. You can conduct a classic lecture in which students take notes throughout. To be most effective, this requires that you frequently remind students where you are in your organizational plan. As the public-speaking adage goes, "tell them what you're going to tell them, then tell them, then tell them what you told them."

If you do not want students to write continually during class, there are other options. You can ask them to write nothing, then make your own detailed notes available after class. However, this can lead to passivity and deprives students of learning the valuable skill of effective note-taking.

There is a middle ground, in which you provide handouts requiring students to take notes, but in limited amounts. Such handouts can contain an outline for the day's discussion, plus skeleton information along with some of the more difficult words and concepts. This saves time in class that you would otherwise spend spelling out "teleology," "punctuated equilibrium," or "semiotics." When you give students an outline it also helps keep you on track, so that you occasionally remind yourself as well as them: "That was point B.1. Now we're moving on to point B.2." The outline gives students some of the information but not all, so that they must still make the effort to write notes of their own.

If you are organized enough to work ahead and prepare handouts for the entire semester, you can have your campus print-shop produce a handout package that students then purchase from the bookstore. Such packages can be relatively inexpensive for individual students, but would be prohibitively costly for you to produce for the entire class considering your limited printing budget. If you choose this approach, check with your department regarding copyright regulations.

You may prefer to post lecture outlines and background on a course web-site, then encourage students to print out the information themselves before class. Alternatively, you can avoid preparing handouts for each session by writing your outline and other details on the chalkboard. One of our mentors filled three sections of the chalkboard before each session with: (a) the lecture outline, (b) suggestions for further reading, and (c) a provocative quotation relating to the day's lecture. To use this technique, you will want to arrive early, and students will need a few moments of class time to copy it down.

If you do prepare lecture handouts, whether for individual classes or for the term as a whole, these can be more detailed or less so. Along with an outline they can contain equations, definitions, words that are difficult to spell or pronounce, and suggestions for further reading. They can contain study questions and lists of concepts you would rather not take class time for students to write. The handouts may also include extra articles, sketches or other images, and a cartoon or two if copyright rules allow.

Teaching Note-Taking

We also find it useful to coach students on effective note-taking, telling them that good note-taking is about finding the main ideas in a monologue or discussion. You can give them short exercises in how to take notes, as we have done at various academic levels. Give your students a paragraph to read or a 2-minute lecture, then ask them to summarize the main idea in one sentence. Ask students for their summaries, and discuss those ideas with the class. You can go a step further by asking students to summarize a main idea and several subsidiary ideas. Our students have assessed the exercise as extremely helpful.

You might also remind students of a basic rule of good study habits: to go home after class and rewrite their notes, or at least review those notes to be sure they make sense. Instructors can encourage this practice by asking, at the beginning of each class session, whether there are any questions from last time.

We may feel that it's not up to us to teach students to take good notes or develop successful study habits. Nor is it up to us to teach students how to write well, how to give effective class presentations, how to think critically, or how to discover their true potential in life. Or is it?

When students have trouble taking useful notes, writing effective English, or speaking in public, it is easy for us to make blanket criticisms of their high-school teachers. But teachers in the school system today have extremely difficult jobs, dealing with huge ranges of academic abilities and language skills as well as students who need numerous kinds of special attention. Rather than criticize, much better for university instructors to take the hand we've been dealt and, in whatever time we have available, give students some structure and guidance for effective learning.

Chapter 30

Employing Audio-Visual Materials in the Classroom

Audio-visual materials are wonderful in the classroom. Whether the format is video, DVD, or film, such materials provide variety, giving students a chance to do something other than listen to you and to each other. They bring another world into the room. Videos, as we will call all such materials for this discussion, can teach many topics effectively by showing interviews with others who have particular expertise or first-hand experience. And because these materials are visual they have dramatic impact. Furthermore, today's students relate well to visual media. However, for all the potential benefits, videos must be used thoughtfully if they are to have pedagogical value.

Each video you use must be selected carefully. It should support your objectives and pique students' interest. Many videos give an informative message but are protracted and dull, narrated in a soporific monotone, or otherwise unsuitable. Look for ones that are compelling as well as informative.

If you choose to show a video, it should play a solid educational role in your class. That does not mean it always has to be serious. A video can take a humorous approach to an issue, or have fun with a topic. But the video should be relevant and informative, and not selected solely for entertainment, or because you are desperate to give students a relief from lecture for a few minutes.

Many of us have made the latter mistake, which reveals a lack of overall class planning and usually produces an unproductive viewing experience.

It is essential that you view a video before showing it in class. One reason is that the video may not live up to its promotion and may not be worth the class time. Another reason is that you need to be prepared to warn students of potentially problematic material. As you can imagine, those of us who have omitted the previewing have found ourselves in embarrassing situations resulting from not having known that a video would contain inappropriate violence, questionable language, or just plain old inaccurate information contradicting what we said in class.

We even recommend previewing videos you have used before. It is surprising how much we can forget from one year to the next. Perhaps the video is less effective than you remember. Maybe you taught the course a little differently this year, and the video doesn't fit. Perhaps there have been fresh discoveries in the field that make it dated. You may still choose to show the video, but viewing it beforehand will allow you to warn students of discrepancies.

Videos for class should be succinct, and previewing them also allows you to select the most useful portion to show. You do not have to show videos from beginning to end. As a general rule, we recommend you show segments of 15 minutes or less, except when they are exceptionally important or informative. Considering how precious is class time, we favour carefully-chosen portions lasting 2 to 10 minutes. This also allows for more variety in class, since you can show such concise segments often during the semester. Viewings should be brief if students are to remember the details in preparation for a class discussion. If you decide to show a longer video, you can give students specific pieces of information to look for, and keep the room sufficiently lighted for them to take notes.

One more reason to preview a video is so you can introduce it and provide any necessary background. It is a good idea to inform students of what they are going to see, why it is relevant, and how many minutes the viewing will take. We recommend giving instructions, or at least suggestions, on what to think about or look for while watching. Remember that the material is new to your students, who may not be aware of the main issues. You might give students several questions to consider while watching, to help them focus and maintain attention. Preparing students helps them derive more benefit from the exercise, and makes for a more successful post-video discussion. It also demonstrates planning on your part, consideration for students, and commitment to transparency in teaching. Our teaching should be a cooperative venture in which students know why they are being asked to do something whether it is watching a video, engaging in a lab experiment, or listening to a lecture.

In my class I sometimes show a 2½-minute video demonstrating that newborn babies who receive physical stimulation later show better physical and psychological development than babies who do not. Before showing the video, I remind students of the definitions of "independent and dependent variables." I tell them that, after the video, I'd like them to identify those variables in this study, and be able to summarize the results, possible confounding variables, and implications for society. It's impressive how much information and how many ideas students can extract from even a brief video if you prepare them for it. —EB

After the viewing, give students a chance to express their reactions. But try to avoid simply saying: "What did you think of the video?" Ask specific questions and have a focused class discussion. You can even design an assignment relating to what they have seen. Some instructors follow a video with a worksheet or group project. However you decide to debrief, to make the visual experience valuable have students do something with it. There are a few exceptions to this rule, such as videos that summarize a lecture or that end on an inspirational note providing an uplifting conclusion to a class session.

If you ask preplanned questions following the viewing, be open to the possibility that you might have missed an important aspect of the experience. Students may have an emotional reaction to a video that you had not foreseen. Or they may have observations, questions, or comments that raise excellent points. Perhaps you have asked your business-management students to watch a video about handling personnel problems on the job; allow students to say that they find the video implausible in its suggested solutions to the personnel problems. Even if you ask students specific questions about what they have seen, give them an opportunity to express other thoughts and reactions. Indeed, you may occasionally decide to use a video relatively open-endedly, asking students to report what they liked or didn't like. By all means, give students latitude to express themselves. But at the same time provide sufficient intellectual structure for them to use their time well and engage in productive learning.

Chapter 31

Using Computer Technology in Teaching

Computer technology has affected teaching as it has affected much of life. With communication virtually instantaneous, and large amounts of information easy to access, technology has created new opportunities, expectations, and challenges for post-secondary instructors.[21] Here are some of the ways you can choose to use computers to enhance student learning, along with some suggestions and cautions.

1. Encourage students to communicate with you by e-mail. As most of us know, e-mail has advantages compared with the telephone, retaining speed and immediacy without the intrusiveness of calls at inconvenient times. It also provides a venue for shy students, who may be reticent to come to your office and speak to you in person. The benefits of e-mail bring a cost, however, for instructors who access their university e-mail at home. We suggest that you decide whether, and in how much detail, to respond during evenings and on weekends. It's important to set reasonable boundaries on your time and on students' desire for instant access. As in any profession, it can also be useful to establish a system by which you respond to e-mail at certain times of day rather than constantly as it comes in.

2. Allow students to e-mail their assignments to you. Particularly if you assign numerous small projects, it can save time and paper and be convenient. Some instructors contend that it eases their workload to read, comment on, and grade assignments on-screen, make note of the grade, and e-mail the assignments back. Not all faculty like this system, though. Some find reading on-screen difficult, and prefer to stick with hard copy.

3. Show imagery or graphics in class to demonstrate various concepts or phenomena, using a laptop and projector. These can be moving or still, and can be from your own fieldwork or from published sources. There are excellent computer simulations for physics, history, medicine, psychology, and other disciplines, available from publishers or from a variety of web-sites. For example, you can find compact disc or Internet sources that audio-visually guide students through anatomical dissections, musical scores, astronomical observations, or economic analyses. Make sure you have practised using the demonstrations and software before bringing them to class.

4. Accompany your lectures with presentation slides projected onto a screen from your laptop. Computerized presentation software such as PowerPoint has become standard at academic conferences, and many professors use it in their teaching. Presentation software, sometimes called slideware, can be useful for organizing your ideas and showing large, easy-to-read summaries as you speak. It can also display charts, graphs, and images in visually compelling form. Slideware is particularly valuable when imagery helps students understand concepts. The software is not difficult to learn or to use. You can also post slides on-line so students can print them out, several per page, and bring them to class.

    However, PowerPoint does have its critics, who say that the system can decrease student-teacher interaction, elevate format over content, and make class sessions appear too prepackaged.[22] Compelling as it is, slideware, when used ineffectively, can actually detract from teaching and learning.

Because presentation slides tend to be so graphically attractive, they can easily become the focal point of lectures and create passivity in students and teachers alike. For example, some instructors prepare slides, then spend class sessions reading them aloud, with commentary, while students sit watching the screen. This tends to be uninspiring and provides little more than what students could derive from a book. Slideware should be just one of many tools in your kit, to be brought out when it is the best way to achieve your objectives.

If you decide to use presentation software, consider employing it only for a portion of any class session, using the screen much as you would an overhead projector. If you do conduct the presentation continuously during class, try inserting blank slides between the content slides, or projecting a relevant generic image when you want students' attention directed at you rather than the screen. Stand close to the screen and remain sufficiently animated and interactive that students are engaging with you. To facilitate the interaction, we recommend you leave the room lighted, so students don't zone out or even fall asleep. Additionally we suggest:

- If you project slides summarizing your lecture, keep the projected points very brief, two or three words each. You can then verbally elaborate, in discussion with students.
- When projecting a slide, give students a moment to read before you speak. Alternatively, project points as a summary after you have discussed them. It is difficult for audience members to read and listen simultaneously.
- When you project detailed material such as graphs and tables, ensure that these are large enough and clear enough to be readable, and project them for enough time (say a minute or more) to be comprehensible.
- If you plan to speak while referring to specific elements of a slide, ensure that you have an adequate pointing device.

- If you post slides for students to print and bring to class, make such slides succinct and brief, so learners will need to think, write, and synthesize during class. (See Chapter 29). When students are given handouts of detailed class notes, they often become passive and may even stop attending sessions.

No technology can substitute for the principles of good teaching outlined in this book. These principles allow you to create the personal connection and lively intellectual exchange that make a classroom come alive. In your sessions the focus should be on you and your students, not the graphics, with learners actively asking questions, making comments, and interacting with you as they cannot with a screen. If you use presentation software, try to keep the focus on the human interaction rather than the special effects.

5. Post your course information on-line. For this you will need access to a web-site. Some instructors create their own. Alternatively, many campus web-sites have links to course web-pages, so that your students can find your virtual course simply by following links from the university home-page. In the old days (a few months or years ago) you could not publish your course information on the web without learning the computer language HTML. Today you can write your pages in almost any standard word-processing program which can instantly be converted to HTML. If you plan to post your course information on the web, you can get assistance from your campus expert, the person with a title something like "manager of educational technology resources." That individual should be able to set up your account on the server, give you the user-name and password you will need, and help you learn the system. You will probably also have departmental colleagues who are experienced and knowledgable on this.

What aspects of your course should you post? All the standard information that you might otherwise (or also) distribute in hard-copy handouts. You might include a course description, the schedule, policies, and assignment details. Posting course material on the web saves printing costs right from the start, and also allows you to update your site regularly without using more paper. You might also decide to give students short assignments in response to a question that you post on the site every two weeks. You might have occasional announcements of which you want all students to be aware. Post these regularly, and require students to keep up. The web-site is also valuable for students if they lose their hard-copy handouts. Your posted course description can also be informative to students prior to a semester, by allowing them to find out in advance about the course.

6. Encourage (or require) students to take part in on-line discussion groups. Such on-line dialogues, sometimes called conferencing forums, occur on sites that you personally set up (or have your university's educational technology expert set up) as part of your or your institution's web-site. You the instructor administer the site and set the parameters of the discussion. So once a week or once a month, you may post a question that you want students to discuss. Individual students respond to it and to each other's comments as well. These interactions are often exciting, and have more students participating than would do so in class discussions.

   Even if participation is not mandatory, the sites tend to receive comments from many students who do not speak up in class. Forums and weblogs are particularly useful for students whose particular learning and speaking styles are such that they do not perform to their potential on short notice in class, but can be articulate and thoughtful when given time to respond in writing. Students who have only been working in English for a short time, for example, can construct their messages slowly and without pressure. One consequence of on-line dialogues is that the instructor has less control over these exchanges than s/he would have over discussions that occur in the classroom. In class, if one comment shifts the group to an unproductive tangent, you can jump in and redirect the discussion; in a virtual setting it is more difficult. As you can imagine, this has unintended outcomes, both negative and positive.

If you choose to set up an on-line discussion, decide whether to make participation compulsory. If so, decide how to grade student contributions, including whether to grade for quality of comments or simply give students points for taking part.

7. Teach your course on-line. There is much discussion today about on-line learning, which is a sophisticated version of distance education. Students are not always at a distance, of course, but may simply be unavailable for your Monday-Wednesday, 2 to 4 p.m., classroom sessions.

    Facilitating learning in a virtual setting is different from doing so in a classroom. Many instructors make the mistake of saying, "I know how to teach, so I can teach on-line."[23] There are several factors to consider: First, when you teach on-line, you do not have a class full of students sitting in front of you. One consequence is that learners have no chance to ask immediate questions, and you have no opportunity for instant feedback. While your on-line course may have an interactive component, much of the work will consist of your giving students information, one-way, which they will access via computer. Clarity of your communication is therefore even more important than it is in a face-to-face situation. Obviously students will query you via e-mail or phone, but this will most often be after-the-fact rather than as part of an ongoing discussion. While you will be happy to take calls on matters of substance, you will hope to minimize calls that are merely for clarification.

    Second, another consequence of the isolation of on-line teaching is that it necessitates more caution and diplomacy. In class if something strikes you as potentially funny, you make the humorous comment if it seems appropriate based on the previous comments, your body language, and the rapport you have with the class. If you spice up your on-line notes with a joke, it can more easily be misinterpreted and get you into trouble.

Third, the materials that you develop (and that students will read on-screen) must be designed for maximum readability and accessibility. Reading on-screen can be difficult. Therefore it helps if on-screen information is chunked in sizes which can be easily managed by readers. For example, you probably want a smaller number of words per screen, and you may want shorter paragraphs and more frequent spacing than you would on the printed page. The instructor must also carefully organize the overall material, which might consist of 100 pages of information. How will you input it so students can access and digest it most easily? How will you use graphics effectively? How will you make it print-friendly?

When designing on-line courses, consult a campus technology professional. On-line courses are best planned and executed with a team approach involving you the faculty member and one or more of your university's information-technology experts, who are often experienced teachers themselves.

How Much Technology?

Is it fair to ask students to do Internet assignments and keep up with your web-site when some have limited Internet access? We all believe education should be available even to those who cannot afford personal computers. However, your university almost certainly has computer terminals in libraries or work rooms that are available for student use. Check with your students at the beginning of term to find out how many need to use university computers. Then personally check out the availability of those computers. As long as all students have access, either at home or school, you may feel it is reasonable to require Internet work. If you decide not to require computer access from every student, you can still have an optional Internet course component. That is, assignments can either be e-mailed to you or hand-delivered on paper. Biweekly writing assignments will be posted on the web-site but will also be available in hard copy outside your office every second Monday. And so on.

College faculty have sometimes felt pressure in recent years to use more technology in their courses. Certainly there are good reasons to employ electronic technology in some aspects of teaching. But do not feel pressured to computerize your course beyond what you think is appropriate. Sometimes technology helps us achieve our objectives; at other times it gets in the way. A high-tech course is not necessarily a good course. Students want enthusiastic and fair-minded instructors who make the material come alive, whether those instructors use chalk and a blackboard or computer presentations and web-sites. The essentials of good teaching transcend technology. As always, it is our objectives that should drive our decisions. Based on those objectives, choose and use those technologies that will enhance your teaching and your students' learning.

Evaluation:

Assessing Student Work Fairly

Chapter 32

Do Not Blame Students for Wanting Good Grades

S tudents often seem obsessed by upcoming tests, and can frustrate instructors with "Will this be on the exam?" But we believe it is unfair for us to reproach students on this score. After all, we help maintain a system in which students must achieve high grades if they want to succeed. We too were worried about exams when we were in their places. And increased competition today means it is even more imperative that students earn impressive marks to be accepted to graduate schools, professional schools, and other programs. In our academic system students have no choice but to work, at least partly, for extrinsic reward. Even the most intrinsically-motivated keep an eye on the grade-book if they have academic or professional ambitions.

If we're going to criticize, we should criticize the system. That system rewards students for test-taking skills as well as for knowledge and understanding, and requires instructors to evaluate large numbers of students in short periods of time, thereby encouraging us to employ forms such as multiple choice that may not be the best measures of true learning. However you may feel about this, resist the urge to initiate class discussions on the shortcomings of the educational system (it will only depress students) unless you are teaching philosophy of education. Rather demonstrate to students that you are on their side. Tell them you understand their concern about grades, that you are delighted they have ambitions and that, yes, those dreams may require good grades. Tell them you will do your best to help them understand what is required of them in your course so they can earn the grades they deserve based on how much time and energy they are able and willing to invest.

Compassion is therefore in order when students worry about examinations. However, if students are continually asking apprehensive questions about evaluation, we are probably doing something wrong. We may ourselves be over-emphasizing exams and papers, adding to students' anxiety about evaluation. More likely, we are being vague in our expectations and instructions. Sometimes we hear ourselves warn students before exams, "Everything from class and from the readings is fair game," but students deserve more guidance than that. Here are a few possible tacks to take:

1. Provide students with lists of theories, themes, ideas, and key words to know.

    Students appreciate receiving a study guide straight from the person who writes the exam. Producing such a guide, however, is time-consuming for you and could be judged as spoon-feeding students. As well, bear in mind that if you decide to give students a list from which to study, you are promising that most or all exam questions will involve items from that list. It is unfair to give them a list of topics to study, then test them on different material.

2. Distribute essay questions, some of which will appear on the exams.

    This is a technique that many instructors use. You might circulate 10 essay questions, then choose five for the exam and ask students to write on any three. This approach lowers stress for students. They are aware of the questions; now they just need to study. Students also learn a great deal by studying for all ten potential questions. And you receive higher-quality answers on exams.

3. Provide them with sample examinations from previous years.

Students especially value such resources. Of course if you are using the same, or very similar, examinations from year to year you probably won't want to hand them out. But you may occasionally find that a few students are in illegitimate possession of copies of old exams. In such a case you will have to decide whether to circulate old exams to all students, whether you had intended to or not. You may also want to radically alter this year's test: It is unfair for only a few students to have access to questions they will be asked. If you are new to teaching or to your department, check with colleagues before handing out sample exams from previous years.

4. Ask frequent questions in class of the type you will include on exams.

Consider interspersing lectures with the occasional exam-type question for class discussion. As mentioned in Chapter 13, this can lead to widespread participation, especially if you come to class prepared with one or more questions on handouts or overhead transparencies. So, after speaking about modern architecture for half an hour, you might say: "Here's a question on this topic, of the type I might ask you on the midterm exam." Then: "In what sense(s) was much of 20th Century architecture notably international in its approach?" or "Describe the Bauhaus and its underlying philosophy." Ease students into small groups to address the question, follow up by discussing the issue as a whole class, then move on with the next phase of your lecture. Back at your office after class, file those questions and use a few of them on examinations. Students will be thankful that you are not only teaching them well, but preparing them regularly for evaluation.

You will never completely allay students' test anxiety but if you believe and act as if you're on their side, students will ask fewer nervous questions.

While we are sympathetic to students' aspirations, we also know it is important to set and maintain high standards in grading. Most students want top grades, but only a few deserve them. It is comforting to remember, when we are unable to hand out more than a few As, that many students don't even expect them.

In my first year as a university instructor, I taught in a professional school evaluating education students who were training to become teachers. I agonized over my first group as I sorted out the first- and second-class marks (As and Bs). One well-meaning student had worked hard, but was just a cut below the A students. I could not, in good conscience, give him an A, and was not looking forward to my end-of-term conference with him. Once there, I informed him straight out: "I gave you a second-class mark." I was just about to launch into all the reasons when he shocked me with: "Good. I was hoping for a second class."

In the same group there was a student who was very talented but whose performance demonstrated a number of problems. Though I had a great deal of empathy for him, the best I could muster for this student was a bare pass. I felt badly about it, and told him: "You have tremendous potential, but need to improve this, that, that, and that." To his credit he replied: "You're right. That's all I deserve. I appreciate all the advice you've given me. Maybe next year I can improve." —HR

In summary, we try to follow these general guidelines regarding examinations:

- Demonstrate fairness by giving exams that are valid representations of the material covered.
- Describe upcoming exams to students in enough detail that they can know what to expect, including the number and types of questions.
- Show students they can trust us by administering exams that are, in fact, as we described.
- Maintain high standards.
- Convey that we want students to do well on our exams and experience success in our course.

Chapter 33

Evaluation Systems Should Be Transparent

Fairness. That's what students want when you evaluate them. From elementary to graduate school, students are very sensitive to what they consider inequitable grading policies, and say that fairness is one of the most important attributes of good teachers. In our experience, students do not mind the instructor who is a tough grader (university students generally appreciate high standards) as long as the grading is what they would call fair. What's fair?

1. Equal treatment for all students.

   As much as possible, we want to deal with all students equally, and not treat some more leniently than others. Make sure you are not being, or appearing to be, partial to those you have known in previous classes, those whose opinions agree with yours, or members of identifiable groups.

   Achieving equity is a more difficult task than outsiders might think. Is it fair or unfair to give a student a poor mark on a badly-organized paper that also happens to disagree with your position on an issue? Is it fair or unfair to give a low participation mark to a student who attends class regularly but does not offer comments due to extreme shyness? Is it fair or unfair to fail a student for poor writing on philosophy or geography papers when that student has only been living and working in English for a year? Is it fair or unfair to give less-accomplished students points for significant improvement throughout a semester, rather than solely judging intellectual achievement? As well, we all have our personal preferences, and groups to which we feel more affinity than others:

Because I did my undergraduate work in my 30s, I am particularly sympathetic to older students, to the sacrifices they have had to make to be in college, to the loss of status they have suffered in becoming beginners again. As well, I feel strong empathy for students from disadvantaged groups who need education and confidence. In dealing with such students, I have to be careful not to treat them more "fairly" than others! —EB

2. Clarity of expectations.

We should lay out rules and expectations clearly, then abide by them. Students sometimes complain that instructors direct them to "use their own judgment" or "be creative" in term projects or on examinations, then give them Cs, Ds, or Fs because the papers or test answers didn't meet some hidden criteria. Students should not have to guess about rules or expectations.

We should have examinations planned in advance, and written into the schedule, to cover particular prearranged readings and lecture material. Students should be told how long tests will be, what kinds of questions will appear, and whether grammar, spelling, and style will count. Some instructors also give suggestions on how best to answer exam questions. For example, we remind students that, on essay or short-answer questions, they are likely to receive better marks making specific reference to theories, ideas, examples, and phenomena, than by making only general statements.

Assignments should also be clearly laid out at the start of the semester complete with descriptions, expectations, and due-dates. That does not mean the syllabus has to sound menacing. But it should tell students in detail when and how they will be evaluated.

Once we have laid down rules, we should stick to them unless a rule change would make life easier for students. The best advice in teaching is: It is acceptable to change a policy part-way through the semester if the change will ease students' workload. So it may be fine to tell students that a particularly difficult reading will not be covered on an exam, but it is not okay to say that an extra reading will be covered. In other words, it is acceptable to relax rules, but not to tighten them. In general, however, try not to alter rules in mid-semester. Even an innocuous-seeming rule change that on the surface appears to be good for everyone may actually disadvantage some students. For example, a change that results in less work on a particular paper or exam might be deemed unfair by those students who have already started preparing for it.

Instructors must decide on numerous guidelines and policies, including:

- How many exams? What kinds of questions? Will any exams be "open-book" or otherwise allow students to refer to notes?
- How many written papers will students be expected to complete? How much research will be required? What kind(s) of research? How long should the papers be? How strict are your referencing requirements?
- How many other assignments will there be? What type(s)? If assignments allow for student imagination and creativity, how will you grade them? The looser and more creative the assignment, the more challenging the task of grading it, and the more vulnerable you may be to suspicions of unfairness.

3. Caution when grading students on participation.

We should exercise caution in assessing student participation. Many instructors believe that participation grades provide incentive for class members to attend, to speak up with comments and questions, and to complete assigned readings so they can knowledgably engage in discussion. Assigning participation grades sometimes encourages students to attend, but is no substitute for your making the class interesting enough that students want to be there. If you decide to include a participation grade as part of your overall assessment:

(a) Keep it small, say 5%. We believe that more than 10% is too much for most college courses. It is subjective and based on questionable criteria such as attendance.

(b) Tempting as it may be, try to avoid using the participation component to reward or punish students for hard work or lack of effort, or for personality traits. Resist using the mark to adjust grades that seem too low or too high based on your subjective perceptions of students. If you believe effort should be rewarded, build that into your overall grading system in other ways, for example by rewarding the amount and rigour of research.

(c) Tell students clearly on what basis you will assess participation. If you do not, you may find yourself in an argument at the end of the semester, after you gave a student 3/10 on participation and she protests. Even if you award 8/10, you must be able to defend your decision. Make participation as objective as possible, by listing its components in your course outline: "Of a potential 100% grade for this course, 5% will be evaluated on the basis of participation. This will be assessed on class attendance, on whether you contribute to class discussions with comments and questions, on whether you make written contributions to the class Internet discussion group, and on whether you demonstrate your interest in other ways. Participation marks will be docked for persistent talking or other disruptive behaviour in class." You can be even more specific, saying that a full 5/5 participation mark will be awarded only to those who attend all/most classes, and participate meaningfully and frequently on an "independently generated" basis (not only responding to questions but initiating discussion).[24] If you decide to include attendance, that means you will have to record it. This can be troublesome and perhaps counter to the spirit of voluntary attendance in higher education. It may even be against policy in your institution. If you have doubts, check with your department head.

4. Transparent grading systems.

We should judge students either on an absolute or a relative standard, and inform them of that. Which of these you use is one of the first decisions you will make in setting up an evaluation system, unless you have no choice but to follow the lead of your institution or department. If you grade on an absolute standard, you are not overtly comparing students one to another. Rather you are asking whether a particular student's exam or written paper meets criteria and standards that you have set out as constituting A, B, C, D, or failing work. You might outline those criteria very specifically or simply generally. You might say, for example, that A work displays achievement of all primary and all secondary tasks, that B work displays achievement of most primary and all secondary tasks, that C work displays . . . , etc. Of course, it is impossible (and perhaps undesirable) never to compare students to each other, but under an absolute system you are not strictly grading one student against another.

In contrast, grading on a relative standard usually means grading on the curve. This involves assessing all the students' exams or papers, rank-ordering them from best to worst, and counting down from the top to see how many earn As, how many Bs, how many Cs, and so on, according to percentages that your administration has determined.

Grading on the curve has a number of drawbacks. First, it encourages competition among students, who may hesitate to help others when those others' improvement could threaten their own chance at an A. When we were undergraduates, our science labs were full of stories about students sabotaging others' experiments to ease the competition for medical school. One solution to this is not to police university labs, but to foster a spirit of cooperation among students. Grading on the curve can also be frustrating for instructors. When you have an excellent group of students it feels wrong to give a C to a student who deserves a B, just because the curve is considered too high. And the system assumes low expectations, as in cases we have experienced in which departments stipulate that average grades on midterms should be less than 70%.

It is true that grading on the curve takes into account the fact that some instructors give more difficult exams than others, and that their students do not deserve to be penalized. It also fights grade inflation, a real problem in education today.

If you grade students on the curve, either by choice or because it is departmental policy, we strongly suggest you set tough exams and grade exams and assignments rigorously throughout the semester. Then, any necessary adjustments at the end of term will pull grades up, not down. Students will be much happier that way.

Once you have set up a fair and equitable system in which you have confidence, you will find it easier to deal with students who complain about their grades. When this occurs, listen empathetically, but be cautious about changing a grade unless you made an error or a clear injustice was otherwise done.

Ideally, evaluation systems should allow students themselves to decide what grades they will receive. Your system should be transparent and clear so that students can decide (consciously or unconsciously) how hard to work, therefore what grade to earn. Of course it doesn't unfold quite this simply. But as much as possible, their grades should be in their hands, not yours.

Chapter 34

Constructing Exams: Multiple Choice, Short-Answer, or Essay?

W hy do we give examinations? Exams serve three main purposes—one for students, one for instructors, and one for administrators.

- To motivate learning (for students).
- To assess how much learning has taken place (for instructors).
- To sort students and determine which ones should continue in a given discipline or in university at all (for administrators).

1. To effectively motivate students to learn:

(a) Exams must be worth enough marks that students take them seriously.

(b) Exams must be sufficiently challenging to require that students study for them.

(c) Exams must contain questions that primarily test hard work in this course, rather than previous knowledge or overall academic ability.

(d) Exams must contain questions that are logical and reasonable tests of the course material. When questions are surprising and unpredictable, students experience the exams as erratic, difficult to study for, and discouraging.

2. To effectively test for how much learning has taken place:

(a) Exams should be representative of the subject matter and should demonstrate similar priorities of content to those we laid out in the course. If we spend two-thirds of the marine biology course discussing ocean ecosystems and one-third discussing specific cetaceans such as whales and dolphins, then approximately two-thirds of the exam questions should deal with ocean ecosystems, and one-third should deal with cetaceans. The breakdown is less clear on final exams when part of the material has already been tested. If we give a midterm exam, then a cumulative final exam, there are numerous reasonable approaches to take. One is that the final exam be 50%–75% on the material from the second half of the course and 25%–50% from the first half, but with some integrative questions that require understanding of the entire course material.

(b) Exams should be representative of the particular objectives we have had for students throughout the semester. In a theatre course, have we wanted students to understand the historical development of Western theatre, or learn to critique a play? Our exams should reflect our objectives.

(c) Exams should be representative of the cognitive levels we have been working at throughout the semester. Exams should be pitched at the right level of abstraction and difficulty for the learning that has taken place. In a physics course, do we expect students to engage in basic applications of quantum physics, or discuss limitations of quantum physics in describing complex phenomena?

It is probably not fair for us to spend the semester reminding students of the importance of analysis and synthesis, then give them a multiple-choice test at the end.

3. To effectively sort students:

(a) Exams must distinguish among students based on the degree to which they have demonstrated a grasp of the course material. If you give an exam to an academically diverse group of students and they all receive virtually the same grade, it was not an effective exam. There are exceptions to this principle, such as a short quiz on a reading that is given solely for the purpose of encouraging students to finish the reading before class discussion. But in general, tests should produce a range of scores.

Designing Examinations

One decision you will have to make is how many tests to give—whether to have only the traditional midterm and final exam, or whether to give frequent quizzes. Each system has its advantages. Giving a small number of exams reduces your marking load and gives you more instructional time (since in-class tests are time-consuming). On the other hand, organizing more-frequent, smaller-scale tests motivates learners to keep up with the readings, and reduces the pressure on students so they are less worried about each one. When deciding which of the two systems to lean toward, take into account their relative merits along with the particular characteristics of your course, and other factors such as norms in your department.

In designing exams we suggest you use a variety of different types of questions. One reason is to recognize and be sympathetic to students' various learning styles. Some students prefer multiple-choice questions while others freeze up at the sight of them. Some students enjoy writing essays while others cannot organize their thoughts under pressure. Some students have excellent memories for details while others have an understanding of wider issues.

Another reason to use a variety of different approaches in exams is to account for the breadth of objectives we have had in our course. We have probably wanted students to learn some basic terminology in the field, to understand and compare different methodologies, and to evaluate certain theoretical approaches. We may very well choose multiple-choice or short-answer questions to test the terminology, and short-answer or essay questions for the more challenging work.

The following are some considerations to keep in mind when devising various types of examination questions.

1. Multiple-Choice Questions

Multiple-choice questions are often employed in university mainly because they are quick and easy to grade. They also test a wide range of detailed knowledge, and are capable of testing comprehension and application. While it takes time to write effective multiple-choice questions, using such questions is becoming increasingly easy now that textbooks often provide accompanying test banks. Test banks can be useful resources for generating ideas for exam questions, but we caution against adopting questions uncritically. Test-bank questions often need to be edited or rewritten to make them relevant and appropriate to your course. For example, the distinctions between the possible answers may not accurately reflect the way you taught a particular point. Therefore, trust your professional judgment and tailor test-bank questions to your particular needs.

When using multiple-choice questions, we should feel responsible for their clarity and accuracy. Students are rightfully upset when an instructor excuses confusing exam questions because they are from the official test bank. No matter where particular questions originate, we choose to include them. And if those questions are unrepresentative, unclear, trivial, or convoluted, we should discard or rewrite them.

Multiple-choice questions are sometimes used because

they give the illusion of objectivity on the part of instructors, who then receive fewer arguments over grades than they would after a written test. However, if you use multiple-choice questions, do not assume they are objective. We exercise subjectivity in our choice of questions, in their interpretation, and in their wording, any nuance of which can represent a point of view.

If you plan to use multiple-choice questions, recognize that they may be imperfect, and consider giving students a way of telling you that. One useful way to accomplish this is to allow students to comment on multiple-choice questions. In this method, instruct students to answer questions as usual, indicating the correct response (a, b, c, d, or e). If they arrive at a question they feel is unfair in any way—unclear, confusing, ambiguous, with more than one correct answer—they should indicate the best response but also add a sentence explaining their answer. If their answer was wrong but their words were informed and displayed detailed knowledge of the issue, you can give them the mark. Remind students not to explain every answer, please, or they will never have time to finish the exam.

Using this method will take you a little longer to grade exams. However, in our experience, if you have written or chosen your questions well, you will have very few comments to read. Students will nevertheless appreciate having the option, and will recognize it as evidence that you want exams to do what they claim to—measure academic knowledge rather than test-taking savvy.

2. True-False Questions

True-false questions occasionally have their place, and because of their brevity have the advantage of being easy to construct. They are, however, extremely amenable to guessing, since students have a 50% chance of being correct. You may decide to discourage this by penalizing wrong answers, but students find this policy harsh. True-false are especially useful for quick class quizzes. When using them on more important examinations, consider assigning them less weight than other questions because of the guess factor.

3. Short-Answer Questions

Short-answer questions are excellent tools for examining students either on factual information or a broader understanding of the material. But they must be written carefully, as specific questions that require specific answers rather than vague or general ones. For example, a question in anthropology: "What is the basis of zoological taxonomy?" would be better written as: "Describe two factors that form the basis of zoological taxonomy." A question in marketing: "What makes some brand names good, and some poor?" would be better written as: "List one brand name that you believe is effective, and one that you believe is ineffective. For each brand name, give one good reason you listed it as you did." The more specific or concrete the question, the greater the clarity for students and the more confidently you will be able to grade them.

4. Essay Questions

Essay questions allow students to display the broad knowledge they have gained over the course, as well as higher-thinking skills. They are valuable for gauging the depth of students' learning and for assessing students' ability to compare, to explain, to analyze, to amass evidence, and to construct arguments. Essay questions are generally divergent, and answering them often calls for imagination as well as organizational and writing ability. Effective essay questions should give students an opportunity to demonstrate a broad conceptual grasp of the material, to show that they possess specific knowledge, to draw on this knowledge to support arguments, and to work at various cognitive levels. When you write an essay question, see that it requires students to know details of the course material, to put those details into context, to analyze (apply, compare, deconstruct, synthesize, or evaluate) information, and to write well.

Essay questions can also be creative. The following final-exam question was developed by one of our mentors in a course on 20th Century European history. The question presented three biographies of fictional individuals—one German, one Russian, and one English—with details of their lives through the century, from birth to death. Students were instructed to choose one of the individuals and analyze, explain, and elaborate on the events of the person's life in the context of what was occurring in the period and in the place in which s/he lived.[25]

As in this example, essay questions can be extremely challenging for students to answer, and provide an opportunity for the more able or knowledgable students to distinguish themselves. They are also challenging for you to grade. Your grading decisions will include:

- whether to have a check-list of facts, events, theories, etc., that should be mentioned in the ideal answer, and how to give part-marks;
- how many marks to add for a particularly original or impressive analysis;
- how many marks to deduct for (a) failure to answer the question as stated, (b) poor organization of ideas, or (c) poor spelling, grammar, and style.

Because the stakes are high on essay questions, we suggest that students be asked to write several short essays (as brief as a few paragraphs) rather than one long one, and be given some choice of which questions to answer on exams.

In summary, examinations should serve the purposes for which they are intended—for students, for instructors, and for administrators. Designed to fit the objectives of the course, they should be constructed carefully with fairness as the highest objective.

Chapter 35

Grading Written Work

In conversation with us once, a college student related the following story. After writing a term paper that she thought was pretty good, she was disappointed to receive a C. The student went to the instructor's office to ask why the work did not deserve better, and the professor responded: "I gave it a C because it's a C paper." Though we'll never know exactly what was said, the story reminds us that students sometimes feel written work is graded arbitrarily, or according to some hidden standards unknown to them.

The traditional view is that instructors owe students little explanation as to how their work is graded, and that the professor's expertise is sufficient. Needless to say, this doesn't fit the spirit of our time. Students deserve to know why we grade their exams and papers as we do. That does not mean they will always agree with us on our decisions, but we need to establish systems of which learners are aware, and in which we feel confident. This allows us to relax and enjoy our teaching more, knowing that we are being as fair as possible. And it leaves us less vulnerable to students' challenging their grades.

Good systems go beyond intuitive notions that a particular paper deserves an A or a D, a judgment that may be based not only on academic knowledge and experience but on biases such as we all possess. For example, we may want to award a paper an A because the student has a writing style we like, because she cited our favourite researchers, or because he speaks up in class. We may want to give another paper a D because it is untidy or because its theoretical viewpoints are different from those we presented in the course.

We want to avoid such subjectivity. Though complete objectivity may be impossible, we strive for what we can.

Grading is not an exact science. However, we can ensure that assessments we make of students' papers are based on a clearly defined set of criteria. This can be done by listing all the features you are looking for in a particular group of papers. These may include the quality of analysis, organization, and writing, as well as the presence of certain key content elements that you have identified. A student who fulfils all the requirements to a high standard gets an A, a student who fulfils most gets a B, and so on. An outline of these elements should be available to students, described in the syllabus if possible, so that learners are clear on what you expect, what your standards are, and on what basis you will grade the papers.

A more formal strategy uses what we call criteria sheets. These can be as straightforward as the following, for a 15-point paper:

Research:	_____	(0–5)
Analysis:	_____	(0–5)
Writing:	_____	(0–5)
Total:	_____	(0–15)

While such simple guidelines do not guarantee fairness, they do break the process further into categories, helping us to think out why we grade papers the way we do. With the above criteria, a student who did excellent research and analysis but wrote the paper poorly would not receive top marks but also would not fail. Some assignments can lend themselves to even more detailed criteria. An example is outlined in the table below for a paper on climate change.

Planning and research:

Followed precise instructions
on syllabus.   _____ (0–2)

Drew from recent major
work in the field.   _____ (0–2)

Evidence and analysis:

Fully and accurately defined
phenomenon of climate change.   _____ (0–1)

Specifically described main
contributing factors.   _____ (0–2)

Outlined key elements of
controversy over extent
of climate change.   _____ (0–4)

Analyzed controversy by
comparing and contrasting
research methodologies in detail.   _____ (0–4)

Did further analysis by thoroughly
examining political factors.   _____ (0–4)

Writing and presentation:

Grammar, spelling, and style
college-level?   _____ (0–3)

Paper neatly and professionally
presented?   _____ (0–1)

References sufficient, accurate,
and properly cited?   _____ (0–2)

Total: _____(0–25)

If you decide to use such an approach, be specific when listing
criteria. Rather than: "Defined phenomenon of climate change,"
try: "Fully and accurately defined phenomenon of climate change."

That gives you the latitude to award a range of grades based on the quality of work.

Whether or not you use formally-stated criteria, it is useful before grading each individual paper to skim it first. Occasionally, a student may not have done quite what you requested but instead took a novel (perhaps even brilliant) approach to the topic. In such cases it may be appropriate to apply your criteria flexibly.

It may sound overly mechanical to grade a paper against a list of specified criteria. But if they are stated carefully, such a system can save time and anguish, and give you some measure of certainty about the grades you assign.

Whatever your grading approach, it is difficult to completely avoid making comparisons between different individuals' work. In fact, occasionally comparing papers can provide a useful check on yourself. For example, after judging one paper as 38/50 and another as 40/50, you may want to briefly re-read the two side-by-side to make sure the second really is better. It can also be helpful to peruse the whole pile immediately before marking, to get a sense of the overall quality. This may help you gauge what general standards to apply. If the quality is poor, it is possible you misjudged the students' abilities at their particular academic level, and may want to ease up on your guidelines a little. On the other hand, if the quality is excellent you might occasionally want to tighten your criteria unless you believe this is an exceptional group of students who deserve the good grades.

Many instructors question whether they should include an effort component in their grading system. Most of us would like to reward the student who worked hard even if the end product wasn't stellar. However, if you use criteria sheets, effort is usually subsumed under other points. In the climate-change example above, your judgment on the degree to which the student "drew from recent major work in the field" rests partly on whether she did considerable research.

If possible, grade papers without knowing who the authors are. You can ask each student to type his/her name only on the back of the last page, though you may find students are driven by habit to put their names on the front as well. No matter where students have typed their names, it is a good idea to put sticky notes over them. Even better, you can hand out the sticky notes and ask individuals to cover their names before handing papers in, which will increase students' confidence in the fairness of your grading.

One issue all instructors have to wrestle with is deciding what percentage of the mark to designate to the actual writing. (For more on helping students improve their writing, see Chapter 7.) Presuming you do not teach English composition but rather teach women's studies, geology, research methods, or graphic design, how much emphasis should you put on the quality of students' writing? If a philosophy paper is worth 25 marks, should you designate 5 marks for writing? 10? If you designate only a small percentage of marks to writing, your grades may fail to distinguish between students whose communication skills are worlds apart. On the other hand, your main concern is that students have grasped the discipline-related content and analysis presented in your course.

We support a balanced approach, and give significant but not overwhelming weight to writing quality. This seems to us the fairest way of empathizing with new English speakers and others with weak communication skills—but at the same time recognizing the importance of good writing to both academic and non-academic pursuits.

Chapter 36

Taking Measures Against Academic Dishonesty

As a college instructor, you are obliged to be concerned with the distasteful topic of academic dishonesty. However, such concerns do not have to overshadow the positive aspects of your work. Let students know that you take cheating seriously, make sure they know the rules, set up systems that make cheating difficult, and be resolved to act decisively if such a situation arises. Taking those steps will minimize potential problems, and give you confidence to act should problems occur.

There are two main types of academic dishonesty: cheating on examinations, and plagiarism.

Cheating on Exams

We remember as students being terrified to look up from our exams even to stare into thin air, for fear that a proctor would grab our papers and fail us. Learning is supposed to be an inspiring pursuit, not a fearsome one. To that end, think about the physical environment of the testing room. Students should be seated as far from each other as possible, to allow them to occasionally look up from their papers without being accused of cheating, and so they are indeed not tempted to look at others' papers.

Consider further strategies to discourage exam dishonesty. Without terrorizing students, invigilators—whether yourself, your TAs, or third parties—should show that they are truly vigilant. They can do this by keeping a close eye on the room rather than doing other work. Students who do not cheat want to be assured that you are preventing less-honest students from taking advantage of a lax situation.

If you feel further precautions are necessary, you may want to make up two versions of the exam on different coloured paper, say one green and one blue. Hand them out in alternating fashion, so that each student with a green exam is surrounded on both sides by students who are writing a blue exam. For the content, you can: (a) Use the same exam, but scramble the order of the questions in the second version. With this approach you will need two different answer keys. (b) Actually write two exams (parallel forms), containing different questions but of equal difficulty. However, making up such tests is time-consuming; it is also difficult to ensure that the two are equivalent.

Speak to your colleagues or department head about how to proceed if you believe someone has cheated on an exam. Your institution probably has policies on how you should deal with such a situation. If you catch students clearly cheating during a test, make notes on what you observe. You can then either take their papers away or let them continue writing. But ask them to see you immediately after the exam. Be firm but open to reasonable explanations. Then take whatever measures your institution prescribes. Never hesitate to seek help or advice from your department head or other administrator in dealing with such sensitive issues; their experience can be invaluable.

Plagiarism

There are two main types of academic plagiarism. The first occurs when students use another's words or ideas without attribution. Students engage in this practice for numerous reasons, including a belief that they can get away with it and a lack of confidence in expressing their own ideas ("I could never say it as well as that author did."). However, sometimes students honestly are not aware that they are plagiarizing because they have not been taught proper citation or referencing. Consider giving students a brief presentation on using sources correctly. Define plagiarism and explain that any substantive idea taken from someone else—even if not quoted word-for-word—must be referenced. Many facts should also be cited unless they are common knowledge in the discipline. Demonstrate a few examples of correct and incorrect ways to use the academic literature. Put the examples on the overhead. Point out passages that require referencing and others that do not, and show students how to distinguish between them. Give them further examples to distinguish on their own or in small groups. You can even draw examples from past semesters' student papers, if anonymity is preserved. This is also an opportunity to remind students of the particular citation-style requirements of your discipline or department.

The second type of plagiarism occurs when students acquire whole essays and pass them off as their own. Students can obtain essays from friends or published sources or, increasingly, they can purchase them from Internet cheat-sites. Numerous such cheat-sites exist, from which students can make easy on-line purchases of thousands of different essays.[26] Want a 10-page paper on Mahatma Gandhi's philosophy of non-violence, a 15-pager on Romantic poetry, or a paper on the music of Beethoven? No problem. The papers are often crafted to look realistic, complete with a few grammatical errors. Some even come with draft outlines for those instructors who request them. You may spot some plagiarized passages based on your knowledge of the field and its published work, but more modern types can be difficult to detect.

It is possible to minimize student purchase of term papers by designing innovative assignments that are specific to your particular course material, readings, or lectures. You can ask students to write short papers applying particular ideas from lectures or class discussions to other writings in the field. For example: "Students, for this week's paper, I'd like you to read Jane Goodall's article on her observations of chimpanzees, which is in your handout package, and analyze it in relation to today's lecture on theories of animal behaviour." Alternatively, you can ask for short in-class essays. (See Chapter 8.)

These strategies may not eliminate the problem entirely, however. What do you do when you suspect a student has purchased a paper, borrowed it from a friend who took the course at another college last year, or found some other ingenious way to avoid writing it herself? If a student has lifted a paper from a published source, instructors can sometimes use a high-tech method of determining that. Several sites now exist which allow instructors to input student writings to see whether they match up with any of a large number of published sources accessed by that site.

One venerable low-tech approach that we have found valuable is the following: If you suspect a student has submitted a paper s/he did not write, call the student into your office as soon as possible after the paper is handed in, and ask him detailed questions about it. What is his paper about? Exactly how did he do the research? What were his main conclusions? What were her chief challenges in doing the research and in writing the paper? What would she do differently next time? What did she enjoy most about writing it? A student who did not write the paper will be unable to discuss it more than superficially. When using this method you will occasionally discover to your surprise that the student actually did write the paper. This may be momentarily embarrassing. But as long as you had reasonable grounds for suspicion, most students will understand. Just apologize and move on.

We do not want to focus on the negative in our work. Besides, we take the attitude that while a student may occasionally cheat in our course and not get caught, the behaviour will catch up with the individual eventually. Meanwhile, if we take reasonable precautions we can minimize cheating, and when it occasionally occurs we can respond appropriately. We can then relax and hone in on the positive aspects of university teaching.

Conclusion:

Reflecting On
Our Teaching

Chapter 37

When Feeling Stale or Stressed, Remember the Essentials

We all know when a class isn't going as well as we would like. Such situations are demoralizing and decrease our motivation as well as that of our students. When it happens—and it happens to all of us—there are remedial steps we can take, even in mid-semester. Here are a few suggestions.

1. List what seem to be the problems.

    Is the class noisy? On the other hand, is it lifeless? Is the class too big, or the room inappropriate? Are you using a textbook or readings that you don't like? Are you part of a teaching team that is dysfunctional? Have you taught this course too often and lost your enthusiasm for the material? Conversely, is this your first time teaching a high-content course, and you're barely one step ahead of the students? Did you get off on the wrong foot by allowing disruptive students to set the tone of the class? Or is it a quiet group that you cannot seem to motivate? Is it an 8:30 a.m. class, and either you or the students are tired? Is this a class of students with particular or unusual needs? Maybe it is a weak group that needs extra guidance, or a class of largely non-English speakers, or students who are taking the course under duress, or especially bright students who need more challenge.

2. Restate the problems in a form you can personally address.

If you have listed "Students are quiet and unresponsive," think of it as "I haven't quite figured out how to make this group respond." If you have written "The readings are outdated," think of it as "The readings need to be updated." While the problem may indeed be someone else's fault, envision it as something you can influence. Take whatever responsibility you can, which gives you the power to do something about it. An insight from psychology is relevant here: If you believe a situation is out of your control, it will be.

3. Review the teaching essentials.

Are the problems related primarily to: (a) course planning, (b) individual lecture planning, (c) communication, (d) management, or (e) evaluation? Once you have identified one or more of these major areas, use this book, other resources, or your own understanding of teaching to identify more-specific problems. If you believe lecture planning is problematic, do you need to work on organization, transitions, variety, or participation? If communication is the difficulty, is it questioning, facilitating discussions, or using your voice well? Like an athlete whose game is in a slump, go through a mental check-list to see what you might work on most profitably.

4. Devise a strategy for turning the class around.

Any good problem-solving strategy should be concrete and specific. It should contain a few points, but not too many. It should be doable and realistic. And it should have both long-term and short-term components. The long-term goals are your ideas about the kind of class you would like to have. Short-term components are immediate and specific first steps, understanding that you will not completely turn things around in one day. Perhaps your main long-term goal is to have a more participatory class. A short-term goal might be: "I'm going to ask more open-ended questions and plan one small-group activity each week." Perhaps your main long-term goal is that students be more attentive. Short-term strategies might include keeping up the pace of the sessions, monitoring the periphery of the class more often, and dealing decisively with noisy individuals.

5. Pick one thing you will do differently, and implement it immediately.

Perhaps you will say: "I'm going to have a comprehensive, minute-by-minute plan for the lecture," or "I won't begin speaking until I have everyone's attention," or "I'm going to implement one small-group activity in each lecture." Psyche yourself up, and go into class determined to make the change.

6. Assess your progress, adjust, and make more changes if necessary.

As in any process of transformation, after you initiate the change be prepared to check, recheck, and adjust. Perhaps your long-term goal was a worthy one, but your short-term strategy did not get you there. Fine: try another strategy. As motivational research suggests, successful people are those who are persistent.

Chapter 38

Motivating Students

One of our most important tasks as teachers is to inspire and motivate students. We want them to embrace the course material, to enjoy and appreciate our academic discipline, and to be excited about the intellectual life. In our quest to make learning compelling for our students, here are some steps we can take.

- Have a vision, and plan activities that excite us and our students.
- Plan a workload for students that is challenging but manageable.
- Present material in interesting ways, and in a variety of forms.
- Transmit our enthusiasm about the material and about learning.
- Be upbeat and maintain a lively pace in class sessions.
- Give students opportunities to engage personally with the material, with each other, and with us.
- Look for opportunities to relate the material to the real world, especially to the students' real world.
- Praise student efforts genuinely and often; be positive about their ability to learn and understand.
- Evaluate students fairly.
- Show that we are compassionate and that we care.

Chapter 39

In Teaching as in Life, Seek Balance

It is often easier to act in the extreme than to exercise moderation. But to be effective facilitators of student learning we must work to produce classes that are structured yet flexible, and serious yet enjoyable. We must develop balance.

1. Provide a firm organizational structure, but be flexible.

   Ideally we organize class sessions that are purposeful and structured but open to the spontaneous. For example, you might have a nice tight class planned in medical ethics. You have a lecture outlined and prepared, and you have a real-life case for students to discuss in small groups. Then, unexpectedly during your lecture, a student asks a probing question concerning another situation that you had not planned to discuss. Should you encourage the digression? Yes. Keep it brief, but yes. *Carpe diem:* Seize the day!

   Very occasionally, even larger-scale alterations to the course are appropriate:

   I was teaching Music Education as part of my university's professional teacher-training program. One day, four aboriginal students approached me to say the course was interesting, but not very relevant to the teaching they hoped to do back in their communities. We talked about it and made a plan. A few weeks later, they organized and led an entire class session on the music of their culture, allowing us to hear songs that outsiders are rarely privileged to hear. The other students in the class were very touched by this experience. You could hear a pin drop as one of the presenters sang, a capella, a song that had been passed down from generation to generation in her family. This incident reinforced for me the idea that courses, despite being organized and structured, should be open to student input. It can provide some of the most memorable learning and teaching moments of our careers. —HR

2. Seek student opinions, but make most decisions yourself.

There are many aspects of teaching in which we the instructors rightfully make the decisions. The instructor should generally decide what topics will be discussed, in what depth, and in what sequence. While we want to be open to student input, we have the knowledge and experience to determine what is important and to prioritize. We also make decisions about scheduling—when exams should occur, when term projects are best due, and the like. Students' interests should help guide the course. But basic content, course structure, and evaluation are our responsibilities.

When I first started teaching, I was afraid to lead, embarrassed to be considered an expert, unsure of my claim to authority. As a result, I asked students' opinions on everything. I used to hold class votes to see when term projects should be due. Finally, during one such discussion, a frustrated student at the back of the class called out: "Just set the date, would you?" I did, and have never asked students to vote on course logistics since. —EB

3. Develop a participatory class, but exercise leadership.

As an instructor, you have a responsibility to be a guide to students investigating your field. While you should seek to develop a participatory class, do not abdicate your responsibility to show leadership. Class discussions are a prime example. While we welcome contributions from students, we should remain in control of the direction and pace of discussions. We may decide to lengthen or shorten a discussion based on student input. We may hear excellent ideas from students that steer a discussion into new territory. But unless a student-directed discussion is unusually productive, we want to exercise our responsibility to manage and to wrap up discussions when we must.

4. Offer information and ideas without stifling students' own imaginations.

Students need us, their instructors, to ignite their intelligence and provoke them to think about issues. But they do not need us to say everything there is to say on those issues. Perhaps you are discussing the intriguing psychological concept of abnormality. Rather than run through the official definition and problems arising from it, you might ask students to generate a list of thoughts or actions they might consider abnormal, then from that list derive a definition along with associated problems. True, this takes a little longer than lecturing. We wouldn't want to treat every concept this way or we would short-change the curriculum. But instructors should be creating opportunities for students to generate some of the important ideas themselves.

5. Provide students with options, but not so many as to overwhelm them.

This balancing act applies especially to term projects and assignments. Giving students choices encourages them to be more creative and actively involved in their learning, and makes them participants rather than passive recipients. It allows them to explore areas of genuine interest, a welcome counterpoint to exams that usually require them to be familiar with the full range of course material. However, it is possible for instructors to give too much choice, especially when students are new to a field.

Imagine being a student in two different sociology courses. In one, you are asked to write a 10-page term paper as an overview of the political philosophy of Karl Marx. In the other, you are asked to write a term paper on any topic in the course that interests you, any length, and in any format. The first assignment allows for little choice, while the second allows for an infinite amount. You might consider a middle ground, and allow students to choose whether to write on Marx's ideas about politics, economics, or history, or compare his views with that of other thinkers. Try to design assignments that compromise. Give students choices, but not so many that they are overwhelmed by possibilities.

6. Be your warm and wonderful self, but keep an appropriate personal distance.

The best instructors let their natural warmth come out in the classroom and in their wider interactions around campus. Students want and deserve to see the real you. You can smile. You can tell them a little about yourself. Teaching should not be an adversarial activity. On the other hand, we should not try to be our students' best friends. At the end of the day we must evaluate every one of them with a letter grade. Teaching involves an inherent power differential between teacher and student that does not allow for real equality, and that demands you keep some professional distance. Even a small detail such as our choice of clothing can help establish this distance. We recommend a personal appearance that conveys professionalism. Call us old-fashioned, but we prefer not to wear jeans in the classroom, and Harley has often worn a tie.

It is easy for students to develop crushes on college and university instructors. You are a symbol of a world they seek to enter, a key to a door they want to unlock on the way to becoming knowledgable, competent, educated people. Your institution probably has rules against instructor-student liaisons. Beyond that, our own guidelines are simple and common-sense. Don't wear suggestive clothing. Don't make excessive eye contact with a particular student in class. Don't behave in ways that could encourage a student's personal interest in you.

We also recommend the following:

(a) In general, avoid touching students. There are occasional exceptions: Some instructors might naturally express sympathy or congratulations by touching a student on the arm or shoulder. At the completion of an intense professional program, or at the end of a course in which you have particularly inspired a number of learners, one or more may want to give you a hug. As members of a helping profession we don't want to be perceived as wooden or unfeeling, or ignore our genuine compassion for students. Neither do we want to hide from such meaningful moments. Just be careful with the tone you convey.

(b) Try to avoid meeting with individual students behind closed doors. This can be difficult when students have personal issues to discuss. Though perhaps overly cautious, we try to keep our doors open no matter how confidential the topic of conversation.

What should you do when a student comes to you with a personal problem? It is certainly a compliment to be perceived as trustworthy and perhaps even wise. But avoid acting as therapist. You can be a good listener and offer encouragement and support, but—particularly if the student has a serious problem—we suggest you urge the individual to avail themselves of Student Counselling. On many occasions we have personally walked students to the counselling department to ensure that they see someone or make an appointment to do so.

7. Create an amicable atmosphere but a rigorous one.

The most enjoyable classes are those with a friendly atmosphere, in which students and instructors feel they can explore interesting and important ideas together in ways that are gratifying to all participants. Ideally the parties feel they like, and have empathy for, each other. In such classes students and instructors sometimes laugh together, and the occasional light-hearted comment is welcomed and appreciated. If you manage to develop such a class, be careful to also maintain a strong sense of work ethic and academic goals. Avoid letting class sessions break down into entertaining free-for-all discussions that do not meet course objectives. The attitude should always be: We are enjoying ourselves but we're here to learn and be productive.

In summary, teaching asks that we strive for excellence without expecting perfection of our students or ourselves. It asks that we constantly assess our work to see that we are walking the fine lines that constitute good practice. It calls on us to apply the same principles to teaching that we do to everyday life, seeking the complex balance that is the best that we can give.

Chapter 40

Especially for
New Instructors

- Should I tell the class that I'm a first-year instructor?
- How much personal detail should I tell students about myself?
- On controversial issues, is it acceptable for me to state my personal opinions?
- What if I walk into the classroom and students won't be quiet?
- What if they ask me a question I can't answer?
- What if I ask students a question, and they don't answer?
- What if they don't like me?
- How can I tell if I'm on the right track, if the class is going well?
- Is it okay to be friendly with students? How friendly?
- Should I lean toward toughness or lenience in grading? Which is fairer and more motivating?

New instructors have many justifiable fears, and face particular challenges. To those of you in this situation we offer the following guidelines.

1. Reveal enough about yourself to show you're human. But do not be self-deprecating or reveal insecurities that might

compromise students' confidence in you—or yours in yourself. You possess the skills and knowledge to teach, and to teach well.

2. Do not be afraid to be a leader: that's part of the job description. First, show that you expect and require cooperation and maturity. Second, seek student input on policy where appropriate but do not put every decision in the hands of students. Assess needs and make decisions accordingly. Third, be organized and prepared for every class—to provide a firm structure for learning and to minimize management problems. Fourth, exercise your moral authority when necessary. For example, if a student makes a demeaning comment (even if no-one from that particular racial, ethnic, or other group is in the classroom) it is your duty to respond and make it clear that such comments are unacceptable. (See Chapter 2.)

3. Avoid attempting to be good friends with students; the situation makes it impossible. Most of us begin our teaching careers wanting students to be our pals, wanting them to really like us. We soon learn the limitations of this. We can provide a warm and encouraging atmosphere; we can be people they respect. But at the end of the course, we must evaluate every single student with a grade. The nature of the teacher-student relationship makes equality impossible. It is best for us to be as comfortable with that as we can. It takes most instructors a few years to learn to develop a friendly and enjoyable classroom atmosphere but with no-nonsense rigour. Students like us just as well when we do.

4. Aim lectures and assignments at the appropriate level for the group; adjust until you get it right. Just out of graduate school, you are accustomed to detailed discussions of high-level theory and debate over controversies that are of interest only to a small number of people in your field. Do not burden your undergraduate classes with such discussions. On the other hand, avoid sounding condescending. Plan to impart certain

information and discuss certain issues; adapt as you go, based on student reaction. New instructors are often so wrapped up in what they personally are doing at the front of the class that they have trouble monitoring student reaction. If you check the class regularly, you will perceive whether students are lost or bored. If they are neither—just interested and challenged—you've probably aimed about right.

5. Set high standards in grading. Beginning instructors sometimes have trouble attaching crass numbers to students' performance. It's true that evaluating students is one of the most difficult aspects of our work. You have a roomful of likeable people, interesting and interested, full of promise and possibility. Most are motivated. Many are people you hope will keep in touch after the course ends and let you know how their lives are unfolding. How distasteful to tack a number to their efforts.

    Of course it's easy giving someone an A. The real difficulty comes in handing out Ds and Fs. For new instructors this can cause regret and even a little guilt ("Maybe I didn't teach the material well enough . . ."). You did teach well enough. Maintain your standards. You may be embarrassed if your grades come in substantially higher than those of your colleagues. If you are in doubt about how your grading compares with that of other instructors, talk to them or to a department head about it. They will appreciate your asking.

6. Learn from experienced instructors. When you have difficulties with instructional issues, ask colleagues for their views and advice. It is unfortunate how little discussion of teaching issues actually goes on in post-secondary institutions. Coffee rooms should be buzzing with discussion of instructional problems and solutions. There should be regular seminars for debate on teaching strategies. But there seldom are, partly because of the emphasis on research and partly because everyone is busy. Furthermore, most of us are hesitant to admit we have teaching problems. But teaching is complicated and impossible to do

perfectly. Everyone needs a few fresh ideas and approaches once in a while.

How can we learn from other instructors? By asking their opinions on specific problems, by gleaning ideas from their course outlines and assignments, and by observing them in the classroom. (This latter may be more easily said than done; when it comes down to it, many instructors are nervous about having colleagues watch them teach.) You might also choose an individual instructor as a mentor. But be cautious in your choice of mentor: A few teachers are successful in the classroom due to natural talent, but have difficulty explaining why because they have not analyzed the tasks and techniques involved. One more point: By all means learn from other instructors, but in the end develop your own style.

7. Retain your idealism and enjoyment of teaching. We hope you feel that teaching is a noble enterprise. It is.

Appendix

Frequently Asked Questions by Instructors

Course Planning

I teach a high-content academic discipline, and do not have time to teach English usage. But when my students submit papers, I can't believe how poor some of their writing is. Do I have to plan to teach writing skills? What should I do?

Plan to require good writing. That includes telling students that writing is important, and rewarding papers for good grammar, spelling and style. It may also include outlining some of the components of high-quality writing, and directing students to campus resources such as a writing support centre. Model good writing in your own work, with accurate grammar and spelling in your handouts. (See Chapter 7.)

It has happened many times. I give a very good lecture that is informative, provocative, and even a little entertaining. At the end I ask for questions or comments, and students have absolutely none. I would be happy with any sign of life from them. What now?

Course planning should include a vision of the kind of class you want to have and a strategy for achieving it. Ensure that you're giving students the message that you welcome their input. For example, ask for student comments throughout a class session, not just in the last five minutes. When you ask for questions, pause, ask again, then pause again. Show students that your request is not perfunctory, and that you really want to hear their ideas. Stand away from the podium if you like, to minimize the physical barrier between yourself and students. Ask questions that are more specific than "Any questions?" You could point out the controversial nature of a particular theorist's viewpoint, and suggest that some students might disagree with it. If there are still no questions or comments, consider other, non-threatening tactics such as asking them to share questions with each other, then with the whole class. Plan such activities to be an integral part of your course. (See Chapter 22.)

Class Planning

How can I justify taking class time to encourage student participation when I have so much material to cover?

It is impossible for us to cover all potential material. As a consequence, we should relax and look at the big picture of our students' learning. Learning occurs when motivated students encounter ideas that are presented comprehensibly and interestingly, and when they have time to think about and discuss those ideas. It's true that we have a large amount of information to transmit. But if we do not give students at least occasional opportunities to interact effectively with the information, they will develop habits of passive memorization, and get information overload.

We believe it enhances learning if we take class time for student participation, even just a few minutes per lecture. Students display energy and ideas when you create a learning environment that permits that. (See Chapter 13.)

If I'm going to let students speak to each other in small groups, won't it create chaos? How will I get them to be quiet again? And won't they get the impression that they can talk throughout the class?

If you wish to initiate small-group work, give clear instructions so students know whom to talk to and for how long. When time is up, bring the class back together quickly and confidently—with your voice, a few hand-claps, a rap of the gavel, a flick of the house lights, or with any other method that is reasonable and effective for you. Then, do not speak until students are quiet. Make it clear when it is your turn to speak. If necessary, tell students outright that during discussion time or small-group work you want them to speak, and that at other times you will be lecturing, during which you expect them to listen and demonstrate politeness. They'll understand the distinction, and will appreciate having had opportunities for discussion. (See Chapter 27.)

Communication

How do you coax non-participants to say something, especially if they have a long cultural history of non-participatory education?

First, show that you value all comments, and model compas sion and tolerance so that no students will deride others' contributions. Second, develop your own phrases that might draw out reluctant students. We use: "May I hear from someone who hasn't had a chance to speak yet?" "Perhaps there's a different point of view in the room," and "I'm sure someone here has had another experience." Third, initiate exercises in which students talk to each other in pairs or small groups, or write ideas on paper to hand in, which allows even the shyest in the room to take part. (See Chapter 28.)

How long should I let discussions go on?

Once a discussion has started, it is unnecessary and undesirable to let it run until every interested student has had a chance to speak. This is especially the case when comments are becoming repetitive. If your course is specifically a discussion seminar, then student comments and questions are the point of the class, and discussions can be lengthy. But in most university courses in which discussion is supplemental to lecture, allow the exchange to continue for a few minutes, then summarize. "Students, you've set up some useful parameters in which we can think about the material. Keep these ideas in mind as we move on." Let students know that it can be intellectually satisfying to ask questions and frame a debate, and that it is neither necessary nor possible to solve all the problems at once. (See Chapter 23.)

Should I use the so-called Socratic method and ask specific students to answer questions, even if they haven't indicated they'd like to speak?

If you use this method—calling on students whether or not they have indicated they would like to speak—it will probably motivate them to study. The method can be useful in helping students reach logical conclusions, generalize from specific information, and clarify their values. However, we do not recommend using it merely for the purpose of increasing participation or forcing students to do the readings.

We personally prefer gentler motivational techniques, coaxing students to want to take part. If you decide to call on students who do not have their hands up, be kind. Not only do students have feelings, but today's young people are aware of their rights and are increasingly willing to complain if they perceive a classroom situation as demeaning or embarrassing. (See Chapter 23.)

Management

My 10:30 a.m. class is full of energy, but my 8:30 a.m. class is silent. Activities that work well in the later class sometimes flop in the first one. How can I improve the class that's not going so well?

It is true that different classes can possess different character-istics, for reasons including time of day, pivotal personalities in the class who set the tone, or external variables such as the size or temperature of the classroom. Reflect on your own work to determine whether you might be presenting material differently in one class from the other. If you too are tired at 8:30 a.m., you may need to consciously project more energy in that class. In quiet classes it sometimes helps to start a session with an immediate participatory exercise, for example having students talk to each other for a moment about some aspect of their readings. Perhaps the two classes need to be managed differently. You could give the groups different exercises that would appeal to their particular energies. For example, if one or two strong personalities are pro-jecting a cynical or otherwise non-constructive mood in one class, everyone may benefit from more small-group work to decrease the influence of those few.

If your second class of the day is more successful than your first, it may be that you worked out the bugs the first time through. Even when presenting different material in the second class, we relax a little as we teach and often present information more fluidly later in the day. It's a fact of life in teaching; however, more thorough planning for the first class can sometimes help.

How should I handle students who talk persistently, whisper, or laugh during class?

Be clear that you have too much respect for yourself and other students to put up with disruptive behaviour. Teach in ways that discourage such action. Come to class prepared with a well-paced and interesting plan; do not start speaking until the room is quiet; position yourself in the classroom so you can see them and they can see you; pitch the material high enough to keep students' attention; and draw students into the material with your enthusiasm and with exercises that involve them in the learning.

At the start of the semester, point out the rules. Be firm, but take a positive approach and appeal to students' desire to cooperate and use their time efficiently. If problems arise, deal with them immediately. Try not to embarrass individuals, but make your attitude clear. Warn the offending students in private after class. If the problem persists, tell students to leave the room and see you in your office later. (See Chapter 27.)

Evaluation

What do you do when a student informs you: "I'm an A student, and I expect an A in your class."?

Students care about grades these days and demonstrate their concern in various and sometimes inappropriate ways. If you are on the receiving end of such a statement, respond sympathetically but firmly. You have set up a grading system in which you have confidence. It rewards hard work and academic ability in the field. Tell such students that whether they have an academic history of As or Cs, the grade they will earn in your course will depend on how diligently they are willing to work in it. (See Chapter 33.)

Notes

1. For an analysis of the historical roots of the subordination of teaching to research in universities, see Larry Cuban's *How Scholars Trumped Teachers* (New York: Teachers College Press, 1999).

2. Our thanks to Gary Poole of the University of British Columbia, past president of the Society for Teaching and Learning in Higher Education (STLHE), for information on current initiatives to improve university teaching.

3. Benjamin Bloom (ed.), *Taxonomy of Educational Objectives* (New York: David McKay, 1956).

4. Many thanks to David Wirtshafter, professor at the University of Illinois at Chicago.

5. For ideas on critical thinking we thank philosopher Leonard Angel of Douglas College in Vancouver, British Columbia.

6. From *Critical Thinking: A Statement of Expert Consensus for Purposes of Educational Assessment and Instruction*, Peter A. Facione, principal investigator (Millbrae, CA: The California Academic Press, 1990).

7. Paul Thompson, *The Voice of the Past*, 2nd ed. (Oxford: Oxford University Press, 1988), p. 102.

8. For useful ideas on editing, we refer to Bruce Ross-Larson's *Edit Yourself: A Manual for Everyone Who Works with Words* (New York: Norton, 1982).

9. William Strunk, Jr., and E. B. White, *The Elements of Style*, 4th ed. (Boston: Allyn and Bacon, 2000).

10. Wilbert J. McKeachie, *McKeachie's Teaching Tips*, 10th ed. (Boston: Houghton Mifflin, 1999), p. 135.

11. For this assignment idea we thank William Willmott, former professor of anthropology at the University of British Columbia.

12. Thanks for this go to Cara Zaskow, instructor at Capilano College, and Lelia Morey, retired instructor from University College of Malaspina, both in British Columbia.

13. Barbara Gross Davis, *Tools for Teaching* (San Francisco: Jossey-Bass Publishers, 1993), pp. 217–219.

14. For this method we thank Sandra Davies, former assistant professor, Department of Visual and Performing Arts Education, Faculty of Education, University of British Columbia.

15. These are questions that Eleanor uses in her classes. For those of you interested in the answers . . .

   (a) Over a large number of subjects this is generally true. Reasons include that people who would not live together before marriage may take such commitments more seriously than those who would.

   (b) False. Large-scale surveys show almost no correlation between age and self-reported happiness.

   (c) Both of these psychoactive drugs are potentially extremely dangerous. The fact that alcohol is legal doesn't mean it is safe. It is interesting that withdrawal from alcohol can be life-threatening while withdrawal from heroin is generally not.

   (d) In meditative states we can achieve deep rest, but this is insufficient. Humans need to fall into the unconscious state of sleep to survive. As well, according to EEG patterns and other physiological indicators, dream sleep is not particularly restful.

   (e) One hole of golf. In statistical or methodological terms, you are hoping for an unrepresentative sample of both your play and his. The smaller the sample, the more likely it is to be unrepresentative and allow you to "luck out."

16. We thank Selma Wassermann, Professor Emerita of the Faculty of Education at Simon Fraser University, for ideas on effective case-study teaching, from our observations of her in the classroom, and from her book *Introduction to Case Method Teaching: A Guide to the Galaxy* (New York: Teachers College Press, 1994).

17. For a useful discussion of the challenges of problem-based learning, read H. B. White, *Dan Tries Problem-Based Learning: A Case Study*, in: L. Richlin (ed.) *To Improve the Academy*, vol. 15 (Stillwater, OK: New Forums Press and the Professional and Organizational Network in Higher Education, 1996), pp. 75–91.

18. This method is a simplified form of social psychologist Elliot Aronson's "jigsaw classroom" originally designed to establish cooperative learning in ethnically diverse student bodies.

19. Selma Wassermann. *Asking the Right Question: The Essence of Good Teaching* (Bloomington: Phi Delta Kappa, 1992).

20. Carl R. Rogers. *Client-centered Therapy: Its Current Practice, Implications and Theory* (Boston: Houghton Mifflin, 1951).

21. For ideas on using technology in the classroom, we thank instructors Michael MacNeill, Janet Waters, and Chris Gratham of Capilano College, British Columbia.

22. Edward R. Tufte, *The Cognitive Style of PowerPoint* (Cheshire, CT: Graphics Press, 2003).

23. For this and other insights into on-line instruction, we thank Chris Gratham, manager, Educational Technology Resource Center, Capilano College.

24. For this contribution we thank instructor Cara Zaskow of Capilano College.

25. We thank James Winter, Professor Emeritus of the Department of History, University of British Columbia.

26. For valuable information on cheat-sites, we thank instructor Melanie Fahlman-Reid of Capilano College, who has amassed considerable information on detecting and fighting computer-based plagiarism.

Bibliography

Suggested Readings on University and College Teaching

Bates, A.W., and Gary Poole. *Effective Teaching with Technology in Higher Education.* San Francisco: Jossey-Bass, 2003.

Boice, Robert. *First-Order Principles for College Teachers: Ten Basic Ways to Improve the Teaching Process.* Bolton, MA: Anker, 1996.

Brinkley, Alan, Betty Dessants, Michael Flamm, Cynthia Fleming, Charles Forcey, and Eric Rothschild. *The Chicago Handbook for Teachers: A Practical Guide to the College Classroom.* Chicago: University of Chicago Press, 1999.

Brown, Sally, and Phil Race. *Lecturing: A Practical Guide.* London: Kogan Page, 2002.

Cameron, Beverly J. *Active Learning.* Halifax: Society for Teaching and Learning in Higher Education, 1999.

Cannon, Robert, and David Newble. *A Handbook for Teachers in Universities and Colleges: A Guide to Improving Teaching Methods*, 4th ed. London: Kogan Page, 2000.

Christensen, C. Roland, with Abby J. Hansen. *Teaching and the Case Method.* Boston: Harvard Business School, 1987.

Cuban, Larry. *How Scholars Trumped Teachers: Change Without Reform in University Curriculum, Teaching, and Research, 1890–1990.* New York: Teachers College Press, 1999.

Davis, Barbara Gross. *Tools for Teaching.* San Francisco: Jossey-Bass Publishers, 1993.

Fisch, Linc. *The Chalk Dust Collection: Thoughts and Reflections on Teaching in Colleges and Universities.* Stillwater: New Forums Press, 1996.

Gedalof, Allan J. *Teaching Large Classes.* Halifax: Society for Teaching and Learning in Higher Education, 1998.

Knight, Peter, E. Nola Aitken, and Robert J. Rogerson. *Forever Better: Continuous Quality Improvement in Higher Education.* Stillwater: New Forums Press, 2000.

Lieberman, Devorah, editor, Catherine Wehlburg, associate editor. *To Improve the Academy: Resources for Faculty, Instructional, and Organizational Development,* vol. 19. POD Network. Bolton, MA: Anker Publishing, 2001.

McKeachie, Wilbert J. *McKeachie's Teaching Tips: Strategy, Research, and Theory for College and University Teachers,* 10th ed. Boston: Houghton Mifflin, 1999. First published in 1951.

Nilson, Linda B. *Teaching At Its Best: A Research-based Resource for College Instructors.* Bolton, MA: Anker Publishing, 1998.

Pocklington, Tom, and Allan Tupper. *No Place to Learn: Why Universities Aren't Working.* Vancouver: UBC Press, 2002.

Ralph, Edwin G. *Motivating Teaching in Higher Education: A Manual for Faculty Development.* Stillwater: New Forums, 1998.

Index